OMG - We

The

§§§§§§§§§§§§§§§§§§§§§§§

Note to Readers

This is a story, not an advice source. Please consult a competent health professional whenever you are in doubt about your baby's health or behaviour.
The author and the publishers cannot accept legal responsibility for any problems arising out of the contents of this book.

National Library of Australia Cataloguing-in-Publication entry

Author: Mulligan, Paddy, author.

Title: OMG we're having a baby! : the diary of a first time dad /

                   Paddy Mulligan.

ISBN: 9780646563459 (paperback)

Subjects: Mulligan, Paddy.

                   Pregnancy--Popular works.

                   Pregnancy--Psychological aspects.

                   First pregnancy.

Dewey Number: 618.24

Contents

Go Raibh Mhaith agat:

For my wife Kavitha Mulligan. For being the perfect, lunatic pregnant woman that I shared this experience with. Thanks for carrying and delivering our baby so safely into this world.

Here's to our Family's Future.....

What ever that maybe ....

"This is perfect in giving Dad's a blokes perspective as well as a decent source of information. It will also give the girls an idea of what we go through. Funny, informative and a must read. "

"Brilliant. Brilliant. Brilliant."

"A hilarious account of a straight forward pregnancy & a straight forward account of a hilarious pregnancy!"

The Introduction:

Firstly, Thank you for buying this book.

It was borne out of the idea that grew as my wife's belly grew, our baby.

We got married on Jan 5th 2010. In February 2010 she was pregnant. Quick? Yes. Planned? Sort of. We had said we'd like to have a baby, but did not expect it all to happen so soon.

First reaction? I was numb. Happy but numb. The stick showed two pink lines and that meant "Yes".

Optimism isn't a fulltime job. Not for me anyway. When it came to this news, my first thoughts were on what I'd loose and not what I'd gain.

Yes, we're a bit dyslexic us blokes! That doesn't ring more true than when having a baby. We think our life is about to end. Our way of life at least. Infact it's the exact opposite - it's all about to start.

That's how I structured this book though. The end comes first, then the middle and finally the beginning.

One life will begin, one will end.

On the optimistic side : you'll never be lonely again - you have a friend for life or at least a large chunk of it.

You'll sing more often and that can only be good for you!

You'll see the beginning of each day earlier than before. You can sleep when you're dead.

You'll cuddle and kiss, chase and be missed.

You'll be every source of knowledge and every source of fun.

You'll see life through the little one's eyes.

Won't you? Yes, but at this stage, you're just not too sure.

We ended up naming our baby after a tree. That tree will grow up and in turn bear fruit of its own. There's a long way from here to there. The journey to here though, has single handedly been the maddest experience ever.

Like everything in life, the first time to experience something is always the best or at least always more memorable. It's the whole shock factor. Hindsight is a wonderful thing but experience is the best.

You'll make mistakes and in retrospect, could have done things better or differently. Such is life. That's what you're living & indeed what you've created.

If you've forgotten what it was like, or are about to go through this for the first time, then this book is for you.

At the early stage I presumed having a baby would be

like having a dog? You can teach it tricks, cuddle it and take it for walks. The added bonus is it won't be as hairy and it'll look a bit like you.

I wrote this book as it happened, and did mostly keep to the original content.

When we saw those two pink lines, we were happy with the news, but totally under prepared. We had nothing planned, no medical insurance and no clue of what to do next.

So what happens in the Man's head during this process? What does he think, feel, know?

Here's what:

The End

The Early weeks:

When it was definite, the thing you first realise is that you can not tell anyone. Advice tells you that 12 to 15 weeks is the time to go public.

Why? Because miscarriages are common that's why. If less people know then there are less people to tell if something bad was to happen. Plus you can try again, it can all go unnoticed.

Therefore the only people who know are you and your wife !?! So you can't talk about this with anyone. It's a big secret that you don't want to keep. It's very, very strange.

I start to realise that the reality is near. We will have a little person to take care of. *"Oh Shiiiiitt!" P*anic kicks in.

There goes "me time", the boy's nights out, the late night football matches, the long sleep ins, the "doing nothing after work except 'chilln the f out'. But relax I say, there's good as well isn't there?

Isn't there?

Awareness:
Week 1

At first though, the serious stuff is all you can think of: The crying, the nappies, the poo?

The End

On day 1 & 2 I feel weird. I'm excited but can't tell family or friends yet, not even the mates with kids.

I start to look at the way they live: they all seem tired, they carry always bright cloudy blue or pink bags containing baby bottles, nappies, cleaning stuff, powder stuff etc. The Dads seem to go through moments of drinking a lot or not at all. There's the reality that they do not get out much anymore. They talk constantly about their kids, for it's not like getting a dog or a new house. It's a bit bigger than that. This is a new universe, or perhaps the same universe but there's a takeover in place.

> **Watch out boys!**
>
> *No raw fish, no herbal stuff, no soft cheese, no deli meats & there's a metallic taste in her mouth all the time??*

I have babysat before and changed nappies, but this time I won't get to leave with $20 in my pocket and say good bye til' next time. This will be a fulltime gig.

How's the wife?

She does have a bit of a belly - this maybe imaginary, but because you know she's preggers - you think you see a bump. We reckon she maybe 5/6 weeks gone. I haven't a clue. When will the cravings start? Will she puke all the time?

In the beginning, she is excited and goes crazy buying

The End

information books which she asks me to read as well. Words like "uterus", "trimester" even "sperm" and "egg" are not words I really want to read.

Her boobs feel sensitive now or "tender" as the books say. It's the first time I see benefits to this pregnancy thing. But can you have sex in the early stages? I thought it was bad for the kid early and late on?? Not that 'late on' sex really appeals right now. She'll be massive, plus the kid inside will hear everything and probably freak out - it all seems very wrong. I mentioned the bonus of bigger boobs but when does the milk start to form? What if we are having sex and I get drenched by that stuff ? ☺

No thanks, not my thing.....

Apparently though, it's all good to have sex at this early stage. It seems wrong, so we wait a while.

As the days pass, she starts to taste things differently. I bought her favourite prosciutto and bocconcini but apparently she can't eat this anymore ????

That's right: no soft cheese, no raw fish, no deli meats, no cold chicken, no alcohol, minimal caffeine, minimal junk food and more fresh fruit and vegetables. The list goes on, this may get tough for me too, but wait a minute, her nipples are bigger and darker now - the benefits balance out.

The End

Then comes the hatred of things: she now hates chicken and not just the meat but even the thought of it makes her want to get sick. I add chicken to my list of "no-no's". While home, at least. ☺

Being a bloke, the initiative to get doctors organised and the rest is not there. She comes home and tells me we have the following things to do:

> - Get her a blood test to make sure she's preggers,
> - Go check out private hospital as it's the first so she wants to decide on what doctor to go with for the baby, an anaesthetist or something?
> -Scan needed at week 12 but we may do it early.

It's all ahead of me, of her - of us: this is how it pans out ..

The Scan:
Week 7

Today we went to get our first scan. Apparently you don't need to do one until 12 weeks, but we wanted to make sure all was cool & find out how long she's been pregnant.

So we walk in. The receptionist is cold, bored and has zero personality, so we just sit and wait for our turn. The lady comes out, greets us and we go into this clean room. The bed is laid out for the wife with loads of computer gadgets around it.

Behind the bed, is a screen waiting to show us the baby inside, and on the wall in front there is a larger version of this screen for us to both look at. This is the one I've to look at, so I don't see anything I don't want to, as I was to find out.

First, the gel goes onto the belly and a camera type thing is moved around and we see some blobby stuff. This apparently was inside the stomach area and you could see some dark areas in there. One of which being the ovary & the other, [wait for it], the *"gestational sac"*.

What the? Well the ovary is where the egg comes from and the *"gestational sac"* is where the baby starts growing.

Then the lady asks the wife to go and '*empty her bladder*' and come back in for an internal examination. This is why I have to look at the screen on the wall and not the other one. While my wife is away, *"emptying"*, I am left alone with the lady and she asks me:

"*When was the last period then, the 30th of December?*"

In my head I replied " *Eh hello, I don't bleed'n know – I'm the bloke here* ?" but I answer her politely:

"*I'm not sure*", she writes something down anyway.

Then my wife comes back in, is handed tissue and is told to strip off from the waist down and lay on the

9

The End

bed chair thing. The private area is covered by a blue sheet and the lady has a contraption that looks like a mini dildo with a condom on it. I know, I know not the nicest thing to read about, but I am sure there will be worse to come.

Casually she goes to work and I just look straight at the big screen. [Apparently it was really easy to get in there ? - what the ?] ☺

On the screen there is more blobby stuff. The technology is amazing. I've seen PSP games with worse graphics.

Anyway the lady points out the Ovary again but focuses on the gestational sac. This crescent-moon-shaped-dark-patch, apparently has the baby in it. She highlights it with a few clicks on the computer [while the other hand is busy mind you] and zoomed in on the area. On the top right I see a round egg-type thing and this area is enlarged again. I knew this looked like the baby but I stay quiet. Then with a few sweeps around it and a bit more zooming, there comes a view of a tadpole-type thing and there is a beating piece to it: yes the Heart!

My wife held my hand tighter and apparently had tears of joy, but I did not see that, I was fixed on the image and gave out a manly *"Yeah"*.

There it is – the baby. But check out what the lady says:

"Can you see that 'Jelly Bean' thing, that's it, and there is a heart beat".

Jelly Bean?

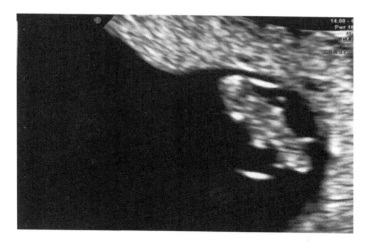

With a few clicks and drags on the screen, she measures the Jelly Bean and it's 12mm long, therefore 7 and a half weeks old!

The heartbeat is measured and comes out normal at 161 beats per minute. That takes me a good ten minute sprint in the gym to get my beat that high but this Jelly Bean is doing that while chill'n out? Respect.

Next the lady starts zooming in on more circular dark bits and measures them. These are the ovaries. The left one is big and round but the other is lost in the blobby visuals. Apparently the left one is bigger because it produced the egg that grew into a Jelly Bean. Good job left Ovary.

The End

On the screen you can see these visuals of fire burning around the black ovary thing and apparently this shows the blood supply that it provides for the bean until *"the Placenta takes over"*.

I'd heard of this word 'Placenta' before but at this moment I could not think what it was and I did not care. Again the visuals of the fire and thoughts of a cool PSP game kick-in.

That's it. The lady records all as normal [even a cyst on the right ovary] and we are free to go !

We collect the Jelly Bean picture on the way out and off we go. The excitement is unreal but I really want to stay relaxed as I don't want to get too excited at this early stage.

> **Watch out boys.**
> *She's starting to crave Chocolate & ice-cream, and wants you to do more cooking & housework ?*
> *The positives: She's the designated driver so you can drink, drink, drink!*

The loss of a baby at this early stage is common, so I contain myself. It dawns on me that the use of the term 'Jelly Bean' instead of 'baby' is probably for this reason: It's easier to lose a Jelly Bean than lose a baby. Touch wood and on we go.

The feeling is amazing. The fact you know all is well is a good feeling. There is a Jelly Bean in there now. Look after it!

The End

Week 8& ½

There were two hospitals needing visiting, so we can better choose which one would be best for us. The GPS is used to get the shortest route and I must time it when I go as well or she told me she'd kill me.

When inside, we had not made an appointment so we pretended we knew where we were going. Looking confident, we looked at the signs near the lift, one saying: "Mothers Postnatal Ward" & the other "Birthing Suites".

Which way do we go? We headed for the "Birthing Suites" and soon kopped on, that this is where the action happened and so did not want to walk in on a woman giving birth. We did though get a sneak peek into a room, it was clean: a bed, instruments and sht.... All good.

The main thing that the girl's are worried about is where they'll stay after – they want the Hilton but you have to go with what you can afford and get the best looking place in your range. Kind of like looking for a decent 4 star room on sale !

We looked at two hospitals, both equally a short distance away, but a peak hour Jelly Bean arrival would make the trip to one longer than the other.

When we looked at the "Mother's Postnatal" places, we met people in the lift with pink balloons and flowers, mother's strolling down the corridors coming from the toilets with their babies in a plastic shopping

The End

trolley type thing , wrapped so tightly, in pink or blue. It was very strange entering this little world. It was like a dream. Added to that we didn't know where we were going. ☺

At one place, the receptionist woman noticed our indecision and we came clean. We had no appointment, we're not here to steal babies and didn't know where we were!

She allowed us to walk the corridors and have a look in, on any open doors. I could see one room where a baby was being washed and the parents were being brought through the finer points of cleaning this little human.

One father, that we met, told us that the rooms on level 1 are the same as these but they don't have a fridge. We were in the Hilton then, and not the Holiday Inn.

In the end, we decided on one hospital. I say we, but it was totally her call. The rooms in one hospital seemed a bit newer so I think that swung the vote for her. This has implications on which Obstetrician she'll choose so let her do the decision making.

Hospital done, how's she feeling?

Being tired has its daily shift:

It starts when she gets to work at 8:30, then she never knows what she wants for lunch, it used to be *"saucy stuff but now dry"*? Then she's tired again at 2:30 till 4. Then home by 6 and tired until bedtime. Watch

The End

out lads the duties are yours now, and this apparently lasts for 3 months !?!

There's a Metallic taste in her mouth and she has to eat all the time to get rid of the flavour. She described it as *'licking the inside of an oyster shell'* – mad !?!

The toilet visits are doubled – she's up and down like a yo-yo: at least 3 times during the night and once every hour at other times?? Lads I hope you are heavy sleepers!

Obstetrician visit 1:
Week 10

We both go to this. I am happy to go at the start, but do I need to go to all these things? I'll plant the idea in her head and see how that goes.

This will be the person who guides us through everything along the way and ultimately delivers the baby. A stranger who will become a very close part of our lives. The decision as to who to choose is based around which hospital is chosen and word of mouth of course.

It's a catch 22 though: on one hand you want to ask people who to use, but on the other you can't tell anyone that you're pregnant.
Yeah ten weeks in and you start thinking more that *"we're pregnant"* and less that *"she's pregnant."*

We are all prepared to meet the Obstetrician, (the Obs), but it turns out he is away. We wait in a room with *"National Geographic's"* and *"Women's Way"*

15

The End

and get called into an office. Here we are greeted by this gorgeous and tall woman who talks very much like a news reader, hair tied up and glasses. Careful lads, not a time to fall in love, especially when the conversation starts about your wife's nipples and expected emotions.

> **Watch out Boys:**
> *She's gone off cooking but that means the cooking shows stop too! More sport lads!*

She is standing in for the Obs we had chosen and is here to explain and confirm all we need to know going forward. First we confirm the expected birth date. The last menstrual period was on 31st of December, so she has this funky yellow wheel thing that has dates around its edges. We are told that the 7th of October is probably the date but we'll add two days for good measure and put in the 9th of October 2010! I try to get another day added on so we'd have the baby on the 10th of the 10th, of the 10th, but I was firmly shut down.

We then enter a questions and answer piece involving questions around how the wife gets dizzy sometimes, about her indigestion and heart burn and we are told all is normal and to keep antacids handy!

We also ask about drinking alcohol and point out the fact that we were both drinking around the new year and wedding celebrations and that this was in and around the time of *"doing the deed"* or *"time of conception"* as the newsreader tells us.

Drinking is generally no good, we are told, but we are

The End

pregnant now and so all things are fine. Drinking is not advised at all during this early part and so the notion of 1 drink on nights out, is actually not a good idea.

This leads me to the great drinking scam you need to pull-off when trying to maintain a social life and keep quiet about the pregnancy at the same time.

> **The Watch Out:**
> *To keep the pregnancy secret at social events:*
> * *Drink the same*
> * *Drink fast*
> * *Swap the glass*
> *& Repeat!*

The Great Drinking Scam:

My wife pretended she was on a "detox" program for a few nights out and this managed to throw the suspicious off our scent.   Excuse two was that she is the designated driver. Excuse three actually involved cancelling dates altogether. Although, the fact that our friends know we are fond of a drink makes it very hard when trying to lie. I kept telling my wife that people are probably guessing we are trying to have a baby or think that we are really boring now as a married couple!

Inevitably though, you can not avoid the social interaction so here's the way around it: You and the wife drink the same drink and you fill hers slightly less than full. Next, you drink yours really fast and leave a bit in it to get ready for the swap. The swap can get

The End

tricky as if someone sees you, they think you are stealing your wife's drink. The chances that someone will notice that you are drinking two drinks, are bigger in your head than what could actually happen. However make sure the wife is helping it all run smoothly. The outcome to all of this is generally one drunk husband and one sober, pregnant wife with a big secret.

Scan Number 2 !
Week 12

Well we walked into the same place for scan 2, past the grumpy receptionist and I am expecting the mini-dildo to show itself again. This has me feeling exactly as awkward as it did the first time.

There is however a bigger issue that has me stressing this time: We are here to do the NT test, [*Nuchal Translucency*]. This will tell us whether or not our Jelly Bean has a high or low risk of being born with Down Syndrome.

What they do is they measure the fluid at the back of the Jelly Bean's neck. If it measures over the average of 2 mm then the risk is heightened. So in we go ...

To my surprise we are brought into a different room this time and there is a different girl there to do the scan. I am told to sit at the head of the bed facing the big screen and my wife lays beside me on the bed. I am expecting the probe stick to come out but I discover that there is no need for an internal check this time as the baby is now big enough to see from an external scan.

The End

The trousers come down slightly, the jelly is put on and the scanner is moved across the belly. The first thing we see is the blobby jelly type thing, that surrounds the black hollow area in the middle. Having seen this already it is easy to spot where the baby lays, and I mean BABY!

The Jelly Bean has well and truly left the building, and the first thing you will notice is the size of the baby: you could easily see the head and body and the legs even. Then the heart beat shows – it is so tiny but beating away. The lady tells us that it is beating at 161 bpm and that this is all normal. I make a joke that the baby is chilling out a bit, thinking the last time it was at a speed of 165 bpm, but infact the speed was exactly the same. Mad the heart has remained beating at the same speed.

The excitement now is brilliant: to see the head clearly and the legs and body and then movement, I ask: "*Is that you moving the scanner or is it the baby?*"*"It is the baby*" she tells us.

I grasp my wife's hand tighter, you can fully see the baby moving and I am not joking the legs were crossed and the Baby was sucking its thumb!

No joke, you could clearly see the hand raised to the face. The nose is visible, the eye sockets – everything! Amazing, amazing, amazing!

It is truly the most amazing thing ever!

The End

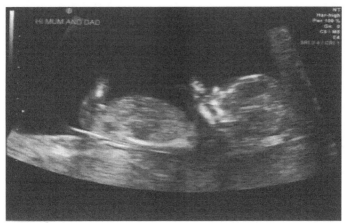

12 Weeks

Surprised by the detail, I ask if in future scans we will have to look away in case we see which sex the baby is. The lady tells us that you need to be medically trained to be able to tell and also that the umbilical cord can get caught between the legs so you may confuse that with the genitals. I think *"I wish my son had genitals the length of the cord"* – but I keep that to myself.

Time to Pray ?

Then the lady goes to work on the measurements and the excitement is lessened a bit to allow her to do an accurate job. The computer races into its measurement mode and the lady drags the mouse from one spot to another at the back of the baby's neck. We silently say a prayer, touch wood and all that jazz.

The scan continues to do cross sections of the baby. You see the brain, and the lady says the butterfly shape is all perfectly normal. All the excitement, shock and happiness returns in bucket loads.

> *The Watch Out:*
> *To see the baby move and the head and body bits so clearly, makes the surreal so real : it's fantastic!*

Next the screen turns on its colours and we see red and blue dashes of lightning hovering over the Uterus. The camera has drawn back a bit and you can see the baby laying down in there and the red and blue flashes look like a weather channel's attempt at illustrating a storm, but these effects are showing the blood flow 'from' and 'to' the baby and the Placenta. The weather is looking really good, we are told to go outside and wait and then we will be called in by a "genetic counsellor". We hug and talk about how amazing it all was: we were not expecting to see that much detail at this early stage.

The genetic counsellor walks from the reception with some papers and has a strange expression on her face. I notice but say nothing to my wife. The pieces of paper would undoubtedly be the blood tests that my wife did the week earlier.

The blood tests and the measurement from the scan [the NT] are used together to calculate the risk level of the baby being born with a syndrome. We are called in and await the result. I remain totally optimistic at this stage as that is all you really can do. Don't count any chickens before they hatch so to speak!

The End

The lady introduces herself – again the news reader/medical voice appears but with an American accent this time.

All the results start. First the intro explains that the NT test is checking for the likelihood of the baby being born with either Down, Edward or Patau syndrome. The lady explains that the risk is calculated as a ratio and that this ratio starts at a point that depends on the age of the mother:

My wife is 31 and therefore starts at a 1 in 542 chance. [for Down Syndrome, the other two are even less likely]. If this was horse racing you would not bet on it.

With the blood test, certain micro levels are measured against averages. The measurement of the fluid thickness was 1.5 mm and is less than the average of 2mm. This is the first time you want to score below average: all is looking well.

Both the bloods and the NT scan results are fed into the computer and the new revised risk is given:

1: 2695!

I know where my money would go now! We are really happy.
The lady explains that if the levels had stayed the same as what we started at [i.e.: 1 : 542] that this would also have been a good result. This makes us even happier.

The results are either good or bad depending on your perception of risk. This result I am extremely happy with, but I can only imagine what a tighter result

The End

would feel like. But all I have to say is to stay optimistic and trust all will be fine. Risk is very low so stay confident in your chances!

When the lady puts these results back onto the computer, the risk level is compared back to an age:

My wife has given the risk results of a 15 year old !?! I am happy but we joke that I could get arrested for such an act!
We laugh and say our good byes: this now means we can get on with the next stage:

The Announcement !

We have arranged a family dinner and pitched it as a 'family get together' to show our recently arrived wedding photos. We have a day and a half to wait so we go celebrate just the two of us!

The wife will drive and I will toast the baby! It's a nice place to be. Proud and allowed: we celebrate!

We were given some photos of the baby from the scan. This time the swap will not be drinks – it will be photographs.

Well the night of announcing is a real buzz. You're excited to tell people so that you can see their reaction, and it means you can break your long kept silence.

This is how it panned out:

I was to sit at the head of the table and after all arrived

23

The End

and the food orders were taken and we all had a drink, [yes even the pretend one for the wife still in place], I would open the photo album and show some photos of the wedding and finally on page 3, I flick the page and there the scan photo's would do the rest.

A few people arrived late for the dinner so there were a few drinks had and the mother-in-law, the future grandmother, was merry by all accounts. Alas the time came, I opened the album showing some photo's of the wedding, then page 2 with more of the same, and then I introduced page 3 :

" *Are you ready for the next page? as these are the greatest photos you are ever going to see.. are you ready..are you all watch'n.....?"......*

Bam! I open the page showing the scan photos and I have to say the reaction on people's faces was amazing : quickly they all knew what was going on, the mother-in-law yelped like a castrated Hyena and the entire restaurant knew we were there!!

The different facial expressions were amazing: all smiled, one yelped, one cried and all were extremely shocked and happy !

Then came the hugs, the tears from the future grand father and more kisses. Dinner arrived to the sound of excitement & shock justification. The relief was beautiful. We could finally enjoy the experience with others.

Surprising to us, all our pretending and swapping drinks, paid off – they had no clue!

With excitement though, came the advice. Everyone

has their anecdotes: don't stretch, no sex, no vacuuming, no alcohol, no cheese etc, etc. You need to remind them that you got this far just fine. The stories come out about their babies and the night sails on...

After informing the family about the number one rule of communication : *"No Facebook"* we closed the night and got ready for the next stage: Telling friends & work!!

Telling work, for my wife, had to wait till later as we needed to make sure all the salary increases [if any] were in place so that we eliminated any chance that they might reduce it when they heard my wife was pregnant and about to take maternity leave.

> **The Watch Out**
> *Telling the family about your future family is the best! The relief and excitement is brilliant: get ready for the advice though!*

This meant a little bit of pretending still had to happen and this was getting harder now as her beer belly was harder to justify at this stage.

The cycle of telling people :

The cycle of telling people goes in stages:

- *First Stage: The Boss.*
- *Second Stage: The immediate family.*
- *Third Stage: The really close friends.*
- *The Fourth stage: B-team friends & Work.*
- *The Fifth Stage: Facebook and beyond!*

The End

The family I told you about. The boss stage relates to me and it's one I'd advise you to tell early on as well. I know it's a little weird that he knows before the clann but it does buy you plenty of half days and flexible hours to attend *"those appointments"*.

> **Lads:**
> *Having a baby is like going to the movies:*
>
> *Expect the worst and you'll enjoy the movie better.*
> *But the popcorn's more expensive.*

With the close friends, we arranged dinners, breakfasts, lunches or Skype sessions to tell them. These are cool too & you do get used to the whole *"news breaking"* announcing techniques.

We used to take turns on who said it, and with some we just said it out straight while others we hinted and then sprang it on them. Skype was a cool medium as all we needed to do was get my wife to stand up behind and rub the flat to petite belly bump.

The B team friends happen unarranged and eventually my wife posted something on Facebook and the job was done. The remaining work people are part of this equation. Eventually you find yourself in a cycle of chit-chat stating the same news to new people. It's like everything in life I suppose : habituation's a bitch.

The Jitters come now:

I was talking to a good friend who has a little girl and asked his opinion on his experiences. He told me that no-one mentioned how hard it is in the first 3-6 months and he went into it laid back and expecting it to be easy. He was smacked with the reality of having a baby, changing nappies, sleeping when the baby sleeps and realising that the freedom that you have before you have a baby has gone.

My message then:
Expect the worst and it won't feel as bad. And more importantly enjoy your freedom now before it all takes place.

My friend also told me that even when he went out for a run, that he got the evil eyes from the wife. He said *"it would have been easier to ask her to go out for a pint"*. Less trouble.

I suppose the hard thing in the beginning is that the baby is not yet human: it does not smile or talk or give feedback. Once that starts it all gets better and better.

Don't get me wrong, I'm not trying to be negative, I'm preparing myself for the reality. The baby is human, it is your flesh and blood, but in the beginning I expect the journey to have a lot of pot holes. If it runs smoothly, then all the better!

The Advice:

Since going public, the cards start coming in now, one read:
" Sleep now", another *" Enjoy the freedom"*

The End

The advice is constant now and is starting to freak me out a bit. All the advice centres around how best to take care of your wife and also on what to expect. The one universal theme that comes, is the inevitable reality that your life will change. Take it all with a pinch of salt, but as you know too much salt can be bad for you !

> **Lads:**
>
> The Obstetrician :
> Make sure you like him/her. The visits are many & they'll bring you Life !

The First Heart Beat:
Week 15

At the 15 week point we had our second meeting with the Obstetrician to do a general check-up: blood pressure, questions, pay $80 and more importantly listen to the baby's heart for the first time.

In order to measure the heart beat, the Obs needs to place a small "glue stick" size contraption to the belly and you can hear the beat through the small speaker out the back of it. The sound is very distorted and sounds like an electrical "wa – wa" like you'd expect from the light sabers in the Star Wars movies. These "wa-wa's" are in fact the heart beats and these are displayed via a digital number on the back of the "glue stick".

The whole thing was rushed a bit. It was our first time to meet the actual Obs and the first impression was

28

not good. He came out of his office to his receptionist and they had a conversation about how delayed they were. We went in, he was not as beautiful as the stand-in girl for starters, and I noticed he had some cuts on his hands. Not something you want to see when you know he'll be using those puppies to bring our baby into the world. I keep all this inside and put it down to first time jitters.

Due to the delays, the Obs answers were all closed. There was little discussion. We were finished in less than 5 minutes. The heart rate monitoring was quick and read around the 161 mark. The service may have been rushed, but the result was the important thing. All was on track and as *"is expected at this stage"*.

The Obstetrician

Okay I had to write this. After our second meeting I decide I don't like the bloke. First up, he seemed pleasant enough but little personality and he just wanted to rush through things and see you next time.

On that visit we arrived with all the excitement in the world, ready to hear the baby and he seemed uninterested in joining in on our excitement. Don't get me wrong he did not do anything that was mean or bad, it just was not what was expected, plus the girl we had met the first visit did seem to be better suited to us. The heart beat was all good, and averaged the same as before and so all was on track.   We headed out to ask a few more questions. With frank and closed answers & a discussion on the blood pressure

29

results [the wife's] we headed out, paid and locked in the next visit. 3 weeks after. All very rushed. For him a process. For us a milestone.

Week 17

The next visit was at 17 weeks 4 days .

We waited for a long time for the Obs on this visit. I had to run down to put more cash in the parking meter and so missed the beginning of the consultation. When I arrived in, the wife was in position, lying on the table with belly exposed and the pants open. For me, this is a real strange sight at this early stage. Especially because the person inspecting my wife is just deadpan. No excitement, all closed answers and all very rushed. I sense he's been doing this job for way too long.

The "glue stick" contraption comes out again and the *"wa-wa"* starts and measures between 145 -151 bpm, which is slower than the last time – but we are assured that all is *"as normal"*.

The first visit we had with this guy, I said nothing about what I thought of him. My wife was so excited about all of this and there was no way that I was going to burst that bubble.

The last thing you want to do is worry your wife. You want her to be totally comfortable with everything.

After this latest visit, I broke my silence with the wife and asked if she was comfortable with everything. This of course encouraged suspicion and she asks why.

The End

I told her that I thought this guy was so boring, had no interest and that I didn't feel comfortable with him. She was still so excited that all the heart beats were at the right speed that she could only reflect loosely on this.

She admitted and remembered been a little disappointed in his short answers.

I eventually brought this up with a couple of mates who have had a kid. They thought I was being stupid but all agreed that we both needed to be 100% comfortable with the Ob's as his/her involvement is crucial and personal going forward.

We decided to explore the options and found a new Obstetrician that was available to fit us in and seemed to have a good reputation.

The thing we realised later was he shared the same reception as Ob's number 1.

Anyway the decision was made to go and meet Ob's number two as I had well and truly blown any comfortable notion that we would use the first Obstetrician. The scabs, lack of excitement & overall bad vibe did not help his cause though. I had no regrets and so looked forward to Obs number 2.

We met the new receptionist [right next door to the other one] and she seemed nice and did all the formalities and in we went.

This new guy was obviously on his best behaviour as he would have known we changed over and presumed we required a certain attitude or certain service. In

The End

short he was a lot more informative, a lot more enthusiastic and much better suited to us.

This guy had a way with words. Sometimes the ladies can not have the baby naturally and so the baby needs to come out a different way : via caesarean or C-section. He described it as a "Vaginal bypass" ☺

If that wasn't funny enough, he also said fk twice! ☺

Even when he was checking the heartbeat he exclaimed: *"never buy anything in China, when the Africans start making things cheaper and their middle class get educated and want more $ the glory days for China are over. "*

There was never a dull moment with this guy. We wanted somebody upbeat, positive and exciting. We got it, plus a bit more: this guy was a little bit mental.

His advice was simple and said with a smile. Regarding food: he told my wife, no soft cheese - unless cooked, no raw meats, and no salad bar due to cleanliness.

He told her: *"Exercise? Go crazy. You can train with the Indian cricket team if u want."*

"Sex. 20 times a day if u want. 21 and it may kill you"☺

I like this guy.

Regarding drinking alcohol, the wife told him she was anxious because she drank like a fish around the time *"of conception"*. He pointed out that fish don't drink and said you'd have to drink throughout the pregnancy to do damage. So all good. Nothing to worry about.

Upon checking the baby's heart beat, he said the beat should be between 110 and 160 bpm.

He then produced this machine that showed a little graph of the beats as it went along. The excitement that we were told about hearing the heartbeat had finally arrived. The heartbeat sounded less like a light saber and more like a heart. Really cool to hear it and more importantly, all was on track with the baby again. The wife's blood pressure was fine and the baby's size was all good. This Obs even had a little DIY scanner to see the baby and that was an added bonus to our visit.

Obs 2 really pulled out all the stops - we left really happy with the news & really happy with our decision. The lesson here is: if you do not feel the 100% comfort and vibe from your Obstetrician, then change !

In hindsight the first Obstetrician was a reputable one, who did not give the service we needed for our first baby. We wanted enthusiasm, excitement and a genuine person who was not overly busy. We have since found out that in the unlikely event that Obs 2 can not be there on the day then Obs 1 will be the substitute. I remain optimistic and we inform the new receptionist who asked why we changed that it was just a personality thing. Enough said I think.

The End

The First movements:
Week 18

It's pretty cool to feel the baby. To her it's like a little flutter inside and can sometimes startle her. The sudden movement can encourage an excited 'Yelp' at the best of times. Feeling the movement though is great – it brings to life the images you have seen in the scan and you can only imagine the little thing kicking or punching in there.

The baby can hear things now and the lower pitch of the man's voice would get through to the baby behind all that bodily noise that it listens to 24/7. It would be like a low bass sound humming behind an orchestra of heart beats and bodily fluids flowing: kind of like listening to Barry White's voice under water.

Have a good feel of the belly, get in there and kiss it and talk to the baby. My wife loves it, and I suppose it gets the baby used to a family sound!

You'll find yourself rubbing the bump a lot & it's a natural attraction, others will also try get a piece of the action but leave that for her to manage. ☺ You try and manage the moods ....

The Moods :

Her behaviour gets full on with cravings now. She ate 4 Chocolate bars the other night and would have taken more. The hatred of chicken is intense now and any notion of cooking it is met with a straight *"No-No"*. While up, she is okay but she now struggles around

The End

very penguin like.

Getting up and off bed or a chair is funny. Do help her up and have a laugh as what that penguin is carrying is now pushing half a kilo and looking for bigger accommodation !

She can't sleep on her back and must be on her side. Apparently it's not advisable to sleep on her right side for too long either?

There will be plenty of moving and moaning during the night so if you have a water bed, loose it now.

Lads
Remember I mentioned the Moods?
They're in full swing now and she can be a right pain in the '#%?!' ☺

The baby inside is now becoming a member of the clan. The movements become a regular thing & occur more and more after a big meal or a big walk. Regular movements are good – it starts to paint the picture of things to come..

Things you'll think about:

The warnings from some parents do crop up in your mind and so they should. Apparently, once you have a baby, even going to the cinema which seems so easy & routine now, becomes an ordeal so big, that it's not worth it unless you get a relative to babysit. So try and stay motivated to go out and socialise. Keep the reality of change on the horizon and optimism in your

The End

head. Enjoy the late nights but get ready for the sun on the flip side - it'll be warm and fuzzy!

My wife had a list one day and on it said *'buy nappies'*. I laughed at it and dismissed it as over-planning. I paid for this laugh later as the duties do start spilling in and the expenses and reality of it all do require your attention.

Boys, the girls are great at moving things along and making quick decisions: don't slow them down but do give your input as it is badly needed. If you leave all decisions to a hormonal penguin you will be left with the egg while she goes off fishing. ☺

The Decisions:

Public V Private:

Think of the:

- Out of pocket expenses
- Comfort
- Own doctor [Obs] - if you're happy with him/her
- Own room-   Is it your first baby?
- I'll say it again – Cash Flow?
- Ultimately – what she wants

Check out both options. Do a tour. If she likes public go for it. If it's your first baby and you are unsure and you can afford it – go private. Remember though they charge you for looking at them.

The End

Names:

The 'Name book' has been added to the collection at this stage and she bombards me with suggestions. If you wish for a boy first up, you concentrate on their names, and depending on your culture, background and what people you admire in life you will get ideas. However you must think of the possible nicknames available, or those school kids will get there first!

Boy v Girl:

If it's your first – you probably want a boy. Well ultimately you don't care as all you want is that jelly bean to turn out to be a fully formed and healthy baby.

But here's the argument , as a Dad, for a boy first up:

If a girl pops out then, happy days you go again. If number two pops out a girl you are in risk of the women taking over the house and listening to that constant mutter of female banter that we can switch off to, but only some of the time. Also if you pop a few girls out in a row – you know in the back of your mind that when it comes to those teenage years that you will have those bloody boys knocking & sniffing at the door.

Plus imagine Christmas dinner – the conversation will be all skewed to the female stuff. That in itself is enough motivation for your prayers. But prayers should finish with the healthy option as number one, gender as number two!

If you have a boy out first – then you know as a father

The End

you have back-up on the male front. He will help with the conversation at the Christmas dinner & ultimately will answer the door to those boys sniffing around looking for *"you know what"* off his little sister.

Also the wife – whether she admits it or not – would probably prefer this order of the sexes as there is an innate human character that craves protection & wants a healthy and strong pack to survive what life will throw at you!

And throw it at you it will! Get ready to catch what you can & enjoy it all!!

The Shopping :
Week 21/22

Alright lads, you know how much the girls like shopping, well this is going to turn it up a notch. My advice from the outset: it's like planning your wedding, let her decide what she wants and look interested for God's sake.

The baby will be an expensive little thing when it comes out, but trust me, that expense starts now. Week 21/22 now and everything, believe it or not, needs to be decided upon now. There is a backorder for everything.

It's like a mini cult these baby shops, you see the women enjoying, talking, discussing & deciding while the men look interested but lost. You can always tell who is having their first cause that look of confusion and expense comes rolling in.

Take the pram for example. It's like a swiss army knife, you need a buggy to walk the baby in right? Yes but the plot thickens:

At the early stages [up to 6 months or so] the baby needs a flat bed, so its bones don't grow bent etc. Then there is an attachment that will seat the baby from 6 months upwards.

> **Lads:**
> *Baby shops have a cult like feeling to them: there is a strong following & you can tell the newcomers!*

Then the car seat comes into the equation: you need one for a new born, but do you get one that comes out of the car and fits into the pram frame or do you lift the baby out of the car seat and just put it into buggy then etc, etc, etc...?

Trust me, you are standing in this store trying to envisage the best way to tackle the baby from the car to the house and vice versa. It is all very complicated but some things do become very clear:

　　　•You need almost 2 of everything,
　　　•You understand the difference between the word 'toddler' and 'new-born',
　　　•You need to get a second job !

The End

From buggies to car seats, to waiting lists, to cots, from bassinets to changing tables and nursery decorations: the whole thing does feel like a storm has hit. Look around the store - this is a world that you are not used to and it is one that will frighten the bejaysis out of you. Take deep breaths, don't decide on first visit & start telling the family what gifts you want for the baby.

> **SHOPPING:**
> *It's like planning your wedding: Let her decide & for God's sake look interested!*

Suddenly the list with *"buy nappies"* does not seem as funny.

The countdown has begun, but how's the Sex? ☺

The Sex ?

Alright she's bigger now. The Ob's has given you the green light to continue sex but what's it like? I suppose it depends on you and the couple you are, but the body of the person is a different body: rounder, firmer belly, bigger breasts and maybe a bigger bum too. There is no difference down there but the major change you'll notice are the nipples. Watch out lads, they are big things and not the most attractive in the world. Cigar nipples galore – but watch what you say – she and them are very sensitive!

> **SEX ? :**
> Yes Please....

One may even be bigger than the other which makes me think it will be the better provider of milk. During sex watch what you touch as you may get a nasty surprise. Anyway, they are so sensitive so the good news is you do not need to work too hard.

The positions are a bit limited and the thought of the baby inside getting disturbed does cross your mind. But sex is sex and is needed: so do it but take it easy boys.

It does become less regular too, this is pretty much due to the elephant in the room: not your wife, the baby. (The fact that she is tired so much & that she looks like she has two arses, [one at the front and one at the back] does probably cool things off.) The love is there though and that's the most important thing.

The End

Middle Earth

Middle Earth

They say sex fk's up everything, well pregnancy is sex's worst enemy. It will slowly kill it. Yes all the stories & all the cliché's are true. It dries up. It's irony at its best. Sex got you into this position but sex won't get you out : it's gone for now.

This may do your head in but don't forget the important thing: Life is coming and you helped create it.

The novelty of the pregnancy does wear off a bit at this middle stage. The bump gets slowly bigger but it is gradual. Just like the grass growing : you don't notice each stage but you do need an expensive lawnmower at the end of it. ☺

You can play games with your wife at this stage. She is not as tired now and has to waddle around very penguin like. I always tell her how beautiful she is, but when she thinks I'm looking for some affection, I have to remind her that I am not into the whole "threesome thing". Joking of course.

Apparently though, there are flashes of hormones during this time, so not all hope is lost. Look out for your window of opportunity.

The 'preggers glow' is there now. I really mean it, she looks amazing. Her skin is perfect, face clear, eyes glowing and the penguin waddle has swagger now. A proud penguin you have on your hands & it's magical !

Her walk becomes more of a bobble and the belly gets bigger but all in all it's *'same old/same old'* at this stage. You continue to do your part and help around the house etc but she and you become used to the whole thing.

There are always reminders and none more clear than when the " Baby Classes" come around ......

The Baby Classes :

Yes you've seen the movies and heard the stories but this time around, it's your turn. If you have experienced the baby classes already then this section is nothing new for you. If though you are reading this beforehand then this is right up your alley. I have kept it as short as possible as there is a whole lot of information thrown at you in these classes.

Most is 'stating the obvious stuff' but there are bits and pieces to take in. The main advantage is it'll give you an insight into what to expect. It is crazy.

Alright there are two options here lads: do the course over two weekends or do over 7 weeknights. Easy decision really but the days are long.

Day 1 for us was called the " Body Shaping " Class. I just remember walking in and expecting it to run all day 9 to 5, but was pleasantly surprised to find out it finished at 3.30 !

The first hurdle was finding the place. As it is at the hospital where you will go for game day, (birth day), I needed to concentrate for this one. That's something that I'm not too keen on. Anyway, we finally arrived, got parked and found where we needed to go by asking a few people in white coats.

We arrived at this abandoned desk and started looking for people. It was quiet with mumbles coming from somewhere and was a bit surreal. It reminded me of this reoccurring dream I used to have of being lost in a more extravagant school that I had attended. White shadows & corridors. Eventually we asked one more person and found that our class had already started. Flash backs from school kicked in again: late for class.

The lady reassured us we had missed nothing and that we find a seat and get our name tags. We did so at the front and sat down.

There are couples sitting around the place. Some girls are alone or with a girlfriend or partner but mostly there is boy/girl, boy/girl.
This middle aged lady introduces herself & straight off we felt she was a funny one. Lucky as what was ahead needs a sense of humour.

The first subject up for discussion was the "mine fields" or common annoyances that all the girls experience. The different suggestions are thrown out and the list is made:

Annoyances:

- People touching the belly
- People saying you're too small/too big
  [not just the belly but the arse as well]
- Horrible birth stories
- Name suggestions and probing
- Breast feeding advice

This all gets the girls talking and sets the scene for the rest of the day: talk about the things in common and talk some more. It does turn into a bit of a 'state the obvious session' but the fact that everyone in the room is going through the same thing at the same time, for the first time does create a buzz.

Next came the emotional & physical changes:

Increased	Decreased
Tiredness	Mobility
Boob Size ☺	Posture
Back pain	Balance
Sickness	Breath
Hair Changes	Memory
Acne - Body or Back	Vocabulary
Calmness	Patience
Appetite	
Toilet Visits	
Sense of Smell	
Leg Cramps	
Cleaning	
Constipation	
Nipple Darkness	

You'll see from above there are no surprises: more than less!

After that, came the Stretches and the old 'Pelvic Floor' talk. Your interest grows here as we hear that when men get older it's important for us to keep the 'Pelvic Floor' strong, otherwise you'll end up in nappies. What a vicious cycle that would be : you start out wearing nappies and you end up the same. I'd rather avoid that.

> *"Pubic Facing"*
> *Just more of the lingo you thought you would never pay to listen to!*

Next, everyone is asked to stand and practice 'Thrusting". I have a look around the room and the sight of all these adults thrusting their hips and smiling is making me feel sick.

You would think things would get better after this, but they don't : these pictures showing the insides of a woman's body, come out. These 1950's cartoon type pictures show the different stages of pregnancy and really show how much the baby squashes up in there - no wonder the wife goes to the toilet all the time!

The lady also explains to the women that when they squat they better not sneeze or there will be trouble. So lads leave the pepper safely stowed away or there'll be pools around the place. ☺

That marks the end of day one and you feel relieved. Good to have experienced this with all the other lads who haven't a clue but tomorrow's Sunday start will start as you may wish a Saturday to finish:

Vaginal Discharge. ☹

Day 2

That's right. Sunday marks the start of the real stuff. At 9 am on a Sunday morning you experience videos and pictures of Vaginas. The very thing that you love is suddenly taken away from you. Please God No!!! Don't let them take this too !

Today, there are bean bags all over the joint so you know you're in trouble. The blokes are encouraged to get involved from the get go, so no falling asleep just yet.

The instructor moves around the room and all the blokes state when their babies are due. She tells us we are not just sperm donors after all. Then she brings on discussion about the baby's position when it's ready to come out. Taking a small doll with Velcro hands, cushion body, plastic head and a plastic pelvis she illustrates the two likely positions:

- Breaching: Bum first
- Engaged: Head first

She illustrates both positions and to my surprise with the 'Head first position' the baby has its face backwards, facing the mother's bum and it comes out using the "pelvic track" as a water slide! The plastic pelvis has bolts on either side and she has to loosen these to push the doll through. In real life, there are no bolts and as I look around the room, the lady's faces clearly show what they are thinking about the task of pushing this baby out a small hole. The blokes, on the other hand, are kind of laughing at this doll being pushed through the plastic pelvis.

The smile is wiped off our faces though, as a picture of

a baby "crowning" is passed around. It's 9 am and we are looking at the top of a baby's head coming out a strange women's vagina. Lads – be prepared.

On the subject of vaginas, I've talked to a few blokes who have had kids and they say not to look '*down there*' on game day, otherwise it will affect your head forever. I think I may take that advice but curiosity killed the cat, and information made him fat: I may just have to look.

The lady next explains that in 3rd world countries they have fewer issues with the baby being in the wrong position. This is because women there do a lot of work while squatting: while they cook, sweep and sit. There are apparently less babies coming out feet first or "pubic facing" [head first facing forward] there. We joke about how the ladies here have it easy but again the photo of the baby "crowning" is not far away so we shut-up quickly to avoid another screening of that.

The DVD goes in and initially I'm looking for the popcorn but soon after I'm looking for the exit door!

Then the talk gets to the actual Labour and we learn that the average number of contractions is 187 – OUCH! and that 1 in 4 women go through Pre - Labour. They're the unlucky ones who suffer for longer and probably bring that average of 187 up and up.

Next there's a DVD played and we settle back into our bean-bags. I'm looking for the popcorn initially but then I want the exit door. The DVD shows women in labour, some sitting on a stool, some squat and some facing forward. The pain is clear but there is an orchestral music soundtrack that helps over shadow that a bit. It does become a bit comical when you hear a chello & piano lightly playing a happy melody, the visual of a woman in absolute pain and a husband/partner in the background looking totally lost.

In one clip it shows a woman giving birth in water and the husband holding her in the bath and being strangled by the wife as she pushes, then the baby is born and no joke, it's PurPle !!

This woman just gave birth to the Joker and the piano is still lightly strumming a happy melody. I won't be getting this soundtrack I can tell you that.

I notice one person who may get the soundtrack though: a bloke is fast asleep on the bean bag. His wife eventually notices and he tries to look interested again. The Joker baby definitely grabbed his attention.   Apparently a lot of babies can appear purple when they first come out, then their lungs kick in and all is well. The baby is given to mammy and she cuddles it into her breast and then nature takes its course.

Darwin was right about evolution it is beautiful but sometimes it does have a funny soundtrack.

The Drugs:

Next the drugs & a tour! .....

" Drugs anyone?"

Yes please! After seeing the video's of women in pain while trying to allow the soft piano music make the scenes better, the thought of Drugs seemed pleasing. Unfortunately there were none on offer and all we had was more discussion.

The lady introduces the fight:

Natural & Medical pain relief in one corner and Pain itself in the other :

Natural	Medical
Visual / Dream	Gas
Massage	Morphine
Heat Packs	Epidurals
Cold Face Cloth	
Music	
Shower	
Bath	
Walking/Moving/Swaying	
Aromatherapy / Oils	
Breathing Slowly / Meditating	

The Natural options, work with the senses to solve pain: sight, touch, sound & smell. The medical options shut down the senses partially or totally. It's up to the wife on this one so she can use all or none. The chances are if the labour is long then she will use a lot of this stuff. So how can we work with the senses? :

The Natural Pain Relief Options:

Sight: Dream/visualise a place or scenario you like and imagine going there. For us boys it maybe at a table in a bar with the lads and your favourite football match on in the background, but for the wife it maybe the African savannah or mystical tree house with waterfalls.

Smell: Oil burners, candles, smelly soaps. Bring them along.

Sound: Music will help with relaxing as will breathing in tune. Music is worth a thousand words so keep quiet and get the playlist ready.

Touch: Massage. Get the oil/lotion and move your hand where the pain is.

> *Drugs Drugs Drugs & No hugs and kisses. Well maybe not.........*

Pack the heat packs and use wet cloths if she gets warm.

If she wants a shower or bath that will help as well. Just ask the midwife first!

Walking, swaying should be good. You may have to hold her up so get ready.

If you are brutal at giving a massage, then my number one tip is to use oil or lotion and this will make it easier for you to feel around the area that the wife wants massaged.   This will make you feel like you know what you are doing and help your wife. Let her guide you to the area and just rub up and down.

Just a note on the music collection, whether it be pop, soft rock or forest/rainfall stuff, try and get it right. I heard one story where a friend cranked the tunes during a contraction and instead of chilled out stuff being played, AC/DC came on. I'm not sure if he's still alive ☺

Failing this Natural stuff there's drugs available:

Pay attention – you may need them too.

The Medical Pain Relief Options:

As with all medical stuff, ask a professional before you consider and don't take the advice of a muppet like me. ☺

1.   First off the blocks is **Gas**. This is the mask you see in the movies that the women breathe in really deeply. It is apparently beside the bed and the levels of gas are controlled by yourself. You may even get to give it a whirl yourself. I think this is only a short-term buzz and a rush of blood to the head type thing. It may not be enough for the wife but she can try it.

2.   Next up is **Morphine.** Isn't this the stuff they give junkies? No that's methadone. I dropped that out in a restaurant one night and everyone around thought we were druggies.

Morphine is a narcotic injected into the muscle. It takes 15/30 mins to kick in and lasts about 2/3 hours. Therefore if the wife is at early labour then this won't be the gig. A longer term fix maybe needed if the Natural and Gas options don't work.

3.   The third medical option is the **Epidural.** This has its risk like any medical operation but it will knock Pain out in the first round.

This involves an injection into the wife's spinal cord, [OUCH], and should relieve pain from the waist down. Specialists will insert the epidural and 'top-up' the dosage as needed by your wife.

Best thing to do around all this stuff is leave it to the professionals, discuss things with your wife and see what happens on Game day. *"It's hard to set a plan for such an unpredictable thing"* as our Obs told us.

After all the drug talk you are bored shitless and need a break. The sleeping husband was asleep again and we watched him get in trouble and stood up. The tour was upon us.

The Tour:

We grabbed our belongings and the realisation that the class room section of the course was OVER !!!!! (It is like hearing the bell at school, the sense of freedom is excellent.) Anyway back to the tour....

The lady walks us down to the Labour Ward and gathers us in a circle and explains that the reception here is where you will check in on Game Day. She explains that there is someone here at all times to answer phone calls and check you into the Labour Ward. I pointed out that there was no-one at the reception and she explained that perhaps the lady was in the toilet. First impressions suffered a bit there but you have to smile and kick on.

Eventually we get the green light to enter the labour ward proper and we walk quietly through.

It's like any hospital and you do get glimpses of families in rooms with blue and/or pink balloons.

Next we enter a room and the lady shows us around. There's the bed with mechanical/medical machines beside it. There are the gas tubes, and some fathers pretend to suck on them. There's the toilet and the bath, (if she wants to have a water birth), and that's it. There's something eerie about touring an empty room. You're trying to imagine what happened in here. The one thing I noticed was that the concrete above the head of the bed had scars on it and I imagined that a women was in so much pain that she scratched those holes in the wall, or she was in so much pain and was punching her husband too much that they had to chain her to the wall and she managed [in the middle of a contraction], to pull the chains from the wall and wow, who knows what happened after that.
Anyway, I didn't share this story with the wife.

That was that, we walked out and we were left to our freedom in the reception. We all walked out together while the course lady tells us to *"have a wonderful life"*.

Walking out we try to imagine the game day arrival and where the car will be parked. If ever the wife needed visualisation practice this was it.

One more day left of this course to do and it was the following Saturday.

> **Day 3:**
> *You're over it at this stage. The dolls are bigger & the topics too real to be entertaining*

Last day – Day 3:

This day started like the last with the introductions, a different lady and the hope that it will all finish soon.

This course was more centred around what to do/expect in the early days of the baby's arrival. Reality check revision is on its way and we begin by splitting the room into two groups. The exercise we are asked to do is write a "to do list" before the arrival. One group has the men and the other women. Needless to say the boys answers are a lot funnier :

> -"Break it off with the mistress"
> -"Rob a Bank"
> -"Pick a venue for the Wetting of the head"

The girl's list was a lot more practical and involved all the material stuff required for the baby:

> - "The hospital Bag"
> - "The Cot"
> - "Bottles", blah, blah blah ...

I won't bore you with the entire list as I've touched off it earlier but this maybe a good time to earn you some brownie points and get the hospital bag sorted [well the easy stuff on the list, get her to do rest:

Here's the necessary:

Easy Stuff	Girl Stuff
Music / Ipod	Lip Balm
Camera	Board shorts
Mints	Aromatherapy Oils
Heat pack	Incense Burner
Pen to write times	Baby Clothes x 2
Toothbrushes etc	Face Cloth
Phones & Chargers	Face Spray ?
Food / Drink	Maternal Pads
Money	Maternity Bra
	Thick Socks

The next thing we had to do was pass around a bag, take one thing from it and the lady would use these items to trigger conversation.

There was a spool of thread to stitch you up - this related to the fact that the ladies may need to get stitching after the birth & for some there can be bleeding for 4 – 6 weeks after the birth? Jaysis - enough said.

Next came a short video and a baby book sales pitch & more discussion on what to expect: No sleep and how to interact.

This third day was a lot more in your face than the

others - more boring but definitely more real.

Then we had to play with dolls. That's right : we all had to practice how to wrap them up nice and warm. This was strange and weird, looking around the room as grown adults all held these dolls, (some even held them all day as if they were the real thing – even some dudes ?).

As we all tried this exercise there was definitely a bit more buzz in the room and you could really see the genuine concentration of people trying to get this right. At the time, it did seem important to do the right thing.

After doll play came another eternal war topic : nappies.

Cloth v Disposable!

This is a real catch 22 as on one side you have the environmentally friendly, dirty to use, clean option & on the other a cleaner to use but rubbish, land filling option.

You choose. I think the latter is the norm nowadays but try get biodegradable if you can. There is even a third option, which the lady shows us. These are funky coloured nappies that are part reusable & part disposable. They have a biodegradable, disposable liner inside. The perfect compromise perhaps ??

I've also heard that in cultures where nappies are not used, the baby learns very fast that the waste it creates is dirty or unwanted. This may only take three to six months. Within our 'nappy wearing cultures', that realisation can take up to 2.5 years. That's a lot of nappies. A lot of waste.

I dream of the day when Nappy companies are forced to make Nappies fully biodegradable. [Not my fight to get that sorted - I'll leave that to you !]

The conversation turns to how best to clean the baby and the lady speaks out very strongly against all these new fancy powders and oils. Her suggestion, back to basics: Soap & Water!

The lady then lays mention to another possible "safety check list" and another "breast feeding" course. I see the blokes getting nervous. This third day has been enough for the lads. The chances of getting us involved in more is not good now. She doesn't try to close the deal so things luckily move on. The next topic is food. There is no mention at all of any products or formula and the lady solely talks about breastfeeding.

It's funny, there is a theory out there that some places encourage breast feeding and others don't. I'm not too sure how serious this is but the whole thing seems to me to be simple. The companies making formula would obviously not encourage breast feeding. It would be a brave Marketing Executive who did.

Again you make the choice on this one. Some women have difficulty getting the baby to feed and some don't.

Apparently the best thing to do is to get the new born baby up to the mother's chest straight away and keep the baby there. This is good for bonding, for feeding, for temperature etc. It makes sense as this is what we would do if we were still a more primitive animal. Gorilla's with less hair. Keep things Natural seems to be the general consensus and I agree.

The lady jokes that there is no nipple preparation required & that instinct will/should kick in. The first load of milk that mammy produces is called Colostrum and this is brilliant for getting the necessary start that will help the baby survive in the great outside world.

Don't worry too much about this stuff. Let the midwives and/or doctors do their thing! Just discuss it with the wife so you know where you both stand on this.

The lady goes on to explain that the stomach of a new born is the size of a marble so it won't take much to fill it. Day 3 it grows to the size of an eyeball, day 10 a ping pong ball and so on.

Then the lady took out a false breast and there was lots of nipple talk.   Picture it : a middle-aged lady with short hair, a strap on boob and 10-12 couples looking on! If aliens were to arrive, right here and right now - I bet they'd do a U-Turn.

Then the lady reiterated that we all need to know that a new baby will be tough but amazingly rewarding and that the wife needs to eat lots of good stuff and lots of calcium! Then we were free to go!

All up there was a lot of good stuff in the courses but you do want to finish them and put them behind you. In one way it feels like over analysis on things but on the other it feels like you don't know enough.

There is too much to know and remember, so just ask the doctors .....

Week 29

It does seem all very routine still. The wife's back hurts a lot more now and she wakes up a lot at 5 a.m. ish. You will definitely be woken up as the shape she is in only allows her to roll, twist legs and hobble to her feet.

> **Movement for Jah People?:**
> Oh yeah! The baby gives the jumper its jump. One kick and you will really feel it

The Big change now [which you will remember vividly from your class's diagrams] is that the baby is now around 1 and a half kilos and as long as a ruler. The little house it belongs to, is getting smaller and all the organs are pushed up and out of its way, so it can move around. Kind of like when we push our pillow away when we sleep.

The whole movement thing is brilliant. The baby is so big that when it moves, kicks and scratches, you can physically see it from outside. The jumper will jump.

There are times in the morning when the hobbler beside you is sleeping and you get the movement all to yourself. This is the greatest thing, the first time you get a one on one with the baby. The kicking or punching is definite & you can feel whether it's a hand or a foot or a leg. You can talk to the baby but this will wake the hobbler. ☺

There are notions that the baby can react to your voice so do give it a go. It will definitely hear and get used to your tone. If you're not shy try lash out one of your favourite songs - maybe the baby will become the rock star that you always wanted to be. Failing that, just read a book out loud.

There is also talk that the baby can see now and tests have been done with torches on the belly. Shine a torch on one side and the baby will move toward or away from it. Sounds kind of cool but I didn't try it to be honest. Sounds like it could freak the kid out. Too early for nightmares.

Apparently the baby can get the hiccups at this early age. The movements are like a regular bass drum beat, perhaps those rock star fantasies are creating a start after all.

She gets really, really restless now – to the point that she has to get up and out of bed. She will try different clothes on and then try sleep again. Watch out she may even raid your boxershorts!

Her emotions are in full swing now. The other day we were going to a baby shop [surprise, surprise] by car to look at designs etc for the baby room. At one stage I got a bit of road rage and looked to my left to find my

EMERGENCY
ALARM

BREAK GLASS
PRESS HERE

wife crying. She was so worked up that I had to turn around and drive home. It was awkward and weird but the only solution was to give her space so off she went and off I went. I returned later with flowers and some sticky date pudding and all was good again.

So watch out and in case of emergency – break glass & oh, get the flowers & chocolate ready !!

The social life now is shorter, but remains the same and you still have a designated driver. The loud bars are not suitable, so you may have to get used to watching the game at home. It is always in the back of your mind however that you should get out while you can. Time is running out, so plan ahead and you'll get your nights out.

63

Time & Money:

The other thing you'll run out of, is money. With all the swiss army baby stuff you have bought or received as presents, you need to look ahead. The wife will not work for 3/6 or 12 months, depending on your situation and you will be the sole earner.

I'm not joking we just moved house, got car, baby stuff & had a look at the finances going forward. The one income will be a struggle & I really could not see a lot of money left over for dinner & drinks. So we will starve and not be able to go out for a while but the baby will be okay. ☺

After looking at this, the reality and the pressure of it all did come to the forefront. My best advice here is, you will manage, you always do. Don't worry too much but do plan to cut spending on going out, luxuries, home delivery & dare I say it beer!!

I had one day of freaking out and then just realised that we will be okay no matter what. A few months of relaxing and budgeting and then we will be back on our feet. So fail to plan or plan to fail? Yeah I suppose.

Do let family members know, and allow them to buy some of the necessary things for the new arrival. There is no use in you buying everything for the baby as you will get presents from people. The family will get some of the big things & friends will get the small stuff :

Big Things	Small Things
Pram	Baby Monitor
Car Seats	Breast Pump
Bassinet	Baby Bath
Moses Basket	Sling / Front Pack
Changing Trolley	Baby Clothes
Cot	Baby Lotions
Mattress	Soothers / Dummies
Portable Cot [Later]	Clothes
High Chair [Later]	Mattress Protector
	Sheets / Blankets
	Safety Products
Nappies ☺	Nappies ☺
Family can help here $$	Friends will help here $$

Don't be embarrassed that you may not be able to
afford everything as there is so much stuff to get that it
would hurt the cash flow of a small business no matter
a small household.

Your wife will probably organise a " baby shower" and
with it will come gifts. My wife even put together a
registry of small cheap things that we needed. This
will help avoid you receiving 9 pyjama sets and 5 pink
blankets.
When the baby shower is on - make plans to go out
with your mates. All this baby talk from the women
will start to do your head in, so do enjoy the times
with the boys.

That is probably the one fact about this whole process
that we need to be careful about. Men are from mars
and women are from Venus but we share the same
Earth. Women will happily talk longer and louder
than men, and this is especially true when it comes to
babies. Leave them to it.
There is one fact that we can never mention to the
women: there are times that we really don't give a sht

about baby bibs, colours for the nursery, breast feeding tips etc. We just want to chill out, watch sport and chill out some more.

There you have it girls – we're here to help but just take it easy on the baby talk & remember that any effort we make is exceptional considering all we want to do is chill out. Thanks for going through the pain of labour but keep the talk for the ladies because Daddy is watching the football.

Best of luck with that one fellas.

My advice: help around, paint the nursery, look interested, then watch the football.

> *Men are from Mars & Women are from Venus….but we share the same Earth*

The Crazy Period:
Week 31/32

Have you heard of Pica? Either had I. According to wikipedia, it is *"characterized by an appetite for substances largely non-nutritive, such as clay, chalk, dirt, or sand"* . According to our obstetrician it is *"Temporary Insanity"*.

Yes my wife is temporarily insane: the latest cravings have been chalk and soap.

It was so funny when she mentioned to our

obstetrician on the latest visits [which become weekly now] that she had these new cravings. He looked interested at first, then my wife said :

" Chalk! and I was thinking perhaps it may be a sign that I am lacking calcium", he was so stunned into silence. The novelty of this was pretty new to him , (and I can only imagine the amount of stuff he has heard over the years.)

Apparently the only thing that stopped her from buying the chalk and eating it was, wait for it:

" You can't eat colours, they must have been out of the white stuff !".

The packs included all colours of chalk and only some white. This apparently, would not have had enough white pieces for her. Even the Jumbo pack had too many coloured pieces. These are the actual conversations you have with your wife. The hormones are obviously all over the shop and they do rub off on you. This all seems quite normal now.

The other craving was soap. I caught her sniffing a small jar of "lux flakes" the other day and she now does it in front of me. Apparently, it was a secret affair she was having behind my back.

One sniff of this for me and I can almost taste soap and it's not nice - she on the other hand can not get enough. It's like a drug for her. Snif , snif. At least it's nothing else she's sniffing. Our friend's baby started copying her the other day. That's how much she's at it.

When I asked my wife about the soap thing, she said

67

she fantasised about biting and crunching into the soap and it making her feel good. *"Crunching"* and *"Chewing"* were said with great satisfaction. This may spring from her love of Indigestion tablets. I swear to God she chews on them like there's no tomorrow. Don't worry as apparently you can have up to 16 of those a day. Don't hold me to that though, read the pack. ☺

When she bought the soap flakes, that are good to wash baby's clothes in, she actually did eat some of it ! I suppose we'll have a cleaner baby.

Really though, I had to tell her this was a bad idea and that the baby would get hic-ups and that bubbles may start flying out her arse, then she soon stopped, (I think). It was back to Orange and chocolate for her.

Throughout the pregnancy though, she did constantly carry this small jar of soap flakes and from time to time I would hear her sniffing it. These ' sniffing sessions', would last a short time each and she told me she even brought the tub into the shower as well. I asked her did she shower in the stuff or eat more of it, and she told me no. I let it go. This temporary insanity will hopefully stop on its own.

She farts a lot now too. I walk into the bedroom, which she usually occupies a few hours before me and the place needs an airing! There's as much methane in this room as you'd expect from a very large cow. Do not call her a large cow though, because you won't survive. ☺

She has major tunnel vision now. All her interests, thoughts and actions are around the baby. It can get annoying but on the plus side, you can also get away with a lot.

Last night she told me she didn't sleep very well. I didn't hear a thing but apparently she was restless, her back stiffened up and she had heart burn. She told me she slept soundly after she took indigestion tablets and said *" maybe I should take these every night before I go to bed ?"* - that's the mentality you're dealing with.

Yes all this temporary insanity can feel permanent at times. Keep the eye contact to a minimum and you may just get through this.☺

Let's face it though, she is entering the latter stages and she is starting to suffer a bit more. Suffer in the sense she is tired a lot more and saying the sicky feeling is creeping back in.

That ' uncomfortable feeling' is always there now and she says she just wants to wear pjs and tracky bottoms all the time.

The intensity of simple things is massive for her. Last night some food fell on the sofa and she freaked out and that mood continued for a while and she was firing all sorts of anger and 'what ifs' at whoever was there. I saw this coming so I commanded the silent position and the sister in law kopped the whole thing.

Week 33

You know women are more active than us. Active as in acting, not as in doing. They want a lot & want it now. Patience is something she has totally lost. If the cupboard needs a fixing or the bulb a changing, then it'll be an immediate, constant and hormone-fuelled demand, that you'll get. She get's stressed over these little things and you'll bear the brunt. Do the jobs, keep her full of chocolate or whatever else she wants and you'll stay out of trouble.

The Cold Shoulder:

The main message is : Don't mess with a pregnant woman, the whole campaign is longer.

You know when you get the cold shoulder off your wife, because you have said the wrong thing, did the wrong thing or just forgot something. When she's pregnant, the consequences are much worse. The silent treatment is far, far longer. I got in her bad books the other day and it took me 3 days to get out. Every emotion is exaggerated , every thought agitated. She can get angry, and it's usually your fault, so watch out ☺

Time wise, we are getting so close now. The nesting has rubbed off on me. I have finished the baby room and all is now done except for the packing of the bag for hospital.

The other night we were watching tv and she could not get comfortable at all. All I could hear was moaning and groaning, then silence and I presumed she was okay, but no she was crying. I asked what was up and she told me she needed an Orange fizzy drink!

Hilarious what? Off I went to the shops and got the drink and all was well. Her back pains and comfort zone were at peace. For now, so was I.

I can tell you what's not hilarious though : Hemorrhoids!

What's that u say? Blood in the poo, argggghhh. ☹ The obstetrician told her to avoid looking at the blood in the toilet as it looks worse as it dilutes through the water. Enough said about that, let's get back to the cravings.

I was talking to my sister about this & she explained her cravings, and likened it to being a junky craving drugs - hers was also an Orange drink. There's a niche market goin on here for those Orange beverage makers!

It all may lean toward the mother searching for her Vitamin C. Nature works in mysterious ways.

The size of her belly is ginormous now. I walked in the other day and she was half naked – the bare belly stood out so much it stopped me in my tracks ..
"Wooooow.... How's it carrying that around all day?"

It was a rhetorical question, the pain in her back is increasing big time now and the load is getting heavier and heavier. The muscles in her lower back are on overtime and looking for a long vacation soon. That is not coming though ... not just yet.

The routine of her hobbling along is habit now, and the only difference is the strain she goes through is always obvious. I try to massage her but I'm no good at it. Send her to the experts, to physio or massage people. Even go along yourself.

As a treat, we both went to a place and chilled in these 'floatation tanks" for an hour, followed by massage. It was the greatest thing ever. Great for her and for you.

Changes

& Expectations:

I'm already noticing the friendship groups changing, the ones that have kids and were always too busy to see you are now ringing and showing up a lot more. It's kind of a club I think.. once you're pregnant you are on the waiting list to join and once the baby arrives you're a member - for Life.

The opposite is true as well. The friends who are single or couples without kids are out more than you and you sense the divide kicking in. When the baby arrives the chances of getting them over for visits or getting out with them will fall. It's life and may take a little while to recognise and get used to.

Real friends will always be there but things change and you can feel it in the air.

The stories from others keep on coming now. The other day my sister told me she met an old friend of mine who has a kid who is 5 months old. His message to me was....

'You don't have to like the thing in the beginning'........... 'all it does is Sht, Cry & Sleep'....
For Dad's, there is little bond there early on.

I am expecting that. The baby in the early stages will be like a little chicken that needs to be fed. Later will come the smiles and animation. Then the fun will start.

These stories and advice captions keep on rolling in. The stories on what sex the baby will be is probably the most frequent, followed by the advice on how to take care of babies, followed by the *"your life is over"* stories..... however these mostly end in a positive way....change will happen good and bad. The good outweighs it. Unfortunately people don't talk about that stuff as much. . Especially us blokes.

Either it's too hard to vocalise or it doesn't exist. Vocalise it I will:

The Beauty...

People don't really talk about the feeling you get when you look into the eye of your own flesh and blood, when you first touch your baby's skin or when looking at your baby's reaction - you see yourself or your wife or even your parents. The curiosity the baby has for absolutely everything is brilliant - from small bits of fluff on the floor to the big blue sky. The world is packed to the brim with loads of beautiful things and teaching him/her reminds you what a really cool world we live in.

These are the things that people don't say. Perhaps it's too difficult to do so. Not everything can be spoken or described - it just is. Experience is Life. Having a baby is like going on a massive trip to Africa [or any destination]. The expectation is there, the excitement is there and the nervousness is there. You want to go, you need to do lots before you get there: pack , injections, read up on, book tours, flights etc etc and when you are there sometimes the experience will not meet your expectations and sometimes it will. You may fight with your travel partner from time to time, you may lose your luggage, you may get lost or even get robbed, but you will see what you see, experience what you experience and have the greatest memories for ever.

Life's not about the past, the future or the present, it's the whole lot mixed together. Having a baby will be like that. I expect the experience to be like our trip to Africa: I expect there to be tough times and I expect experiences like meeting the smiling children of

Rwanda to the curious wildlife of the Serengeti. It is something I will never forget. You need to plan experience, and reminisce later to get the full picture. For now I am at the planning stage of the baby process. Bring on the memories not yet created!

That's why people constantly talk about the bad things in life as it's harder sometimes, to express the good in words. The feelings of being somewhere or having something , can not really be told, they are experienced. The warnings and difficulties are easier to point out as they are concrete.

I suppose then, the baby will grow and bring with it the rediscovery of how beautiful this world is and how far we have come. Today I poured honey on pancakes that I made and visioned explaining where all these ingredients came from – the fact we harvest the wheat to make the flour and that bees gave us their honey to sweeten things along. Things I now take for granted are starting to become beautiful again. The lack of sleep does not seem to be so daunting now, bring it on for I will sleep when I am dead.

Thanks baby.

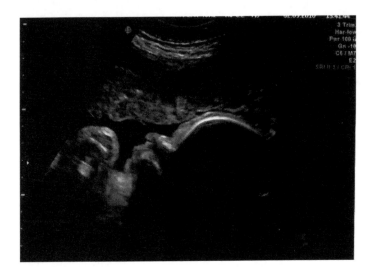

Week 34

I think at this point it is really starting to hit home that we will have a kid really soon. Nothing changes really in our behaviour and she has been pregnant for so long now that the novelty has worn off but that will soon change as we enter the last few weeks I'm sure.

We need to still pack the bag for the hospital and will probably do that this weekend. I have saved the hospital number in my phone and asked my wife's step-dad to be "on-call' when we get to the vital stages, for he'll have to drive my wife to the hospital if I am too far away.

Other than that we're ready to rock n roll. She has to push it out so I can only imagine what thoughts are going through her head.

I don't really bring it up as it's probably best not to acknowledge the elephant in the room, excuse the pun.

My wife is energetic still and constantly writing in her baby book and noting all the memories. She also constantly rubs her belly and the movements are great now. You can totally feel a baby in there.

Sometimes you think you can feel the head or it could be its bum, then you think you can feel the feet or hands – it's really cool. We went to our Obs this week and he showed us the baby was now head down and not "breached" as they call heads up. Engaged they call it.

> Your wife will only talk about
> baby now so be prepared for it.
> It can get a little too much so try
> join in.

This helped settle any doubt on whether or not it is the feet or the arms at the base of her ribs. Sometimes the baby stretches out and my wife yelps as it hurts her. You can totally picture the little baby tucking his/her feet under the diaphragm and ribs and using that as a cushion while it settles into a comfortable position. This though is at the expense of my wife's comfort, so I have to discipline the baby from outside and sometimes it moves. Maybe a coincidence but it's still cool to imagine.

The other thing is when the baby hiccups you can put your hand on there and feel it. Don't try to frighten it to stop the hiccups , they usually go quickly.....

The Babyshower

Baby shower is on in 2 weeks, I think that is a bit later than the norm but I leave that to the girls. I've invited some lads around so we'll head down the pub while all the girls do their thing.

It's something new to me, this baby shower as it's not done where I come from. Friends usually get together after the birth for the Christening or something and give gifts, get sloshed and eat too much food, but this party happens beforehand.

The main advantage, other than getting down the pub with the lads is the gift giving. This is no doubt why this "baby shower" started and has been so successful. Make sure you don't go buying every little thing for your baby as people want to buy you stuff so make a list and put a registry together. You don't need to get involved in that just make sure the wife does it. It will save you money in the long run and I think, it is the done thing?

I'll report back how it all goes later.

The last Ultra Sound:
Week 35

Yes the final ultra sound/scan is upon us. What started as a 'Jelly Bean'" is now a full on 2.5 kg baby. Before this ultra sound I decided to follow the simple "two-step money saving technique":

1. Ring around – get options.   2. Haggle

This applies to anything in life. If you want to save, do it. For all our earlier scans we went with the same place. It is also one of the options that the Obs suggest. Remember when the Obs gives you a 'referral' that is all it is. You can use who you want.

The place we were due to use cost $300. Some of which comes back from the government but it's pricey.

> *Remember your wife has other things on her mind [and in her body] so it's up to you to search and haggle for things. Be the business man*

I unfortunately left it very late to follow the " two-step technique" but I did find places for $200. Due to time though we were forced to use our original place but not before I rang them and tried haggling. I did not get anything off but at least I did try.

For everything previous to this I did not really ring around or haggle. Make sure you do a better job than me ☺

So to the important bit: the scan. We go in and get greeted by the sterile receptionist. We are then pleased to be greeted by the same lady who did one of our earlier scans.
The big watch out in this scan was the, wait for it : "Placenta Previa".

It surprises me that at this stage these silly expressions become part of the vocab. Basically this "P.P." exists when the Placenta [which is the baby's restaurant] is blocking the way out the door. If the Placenta is anywhere near the exit door then the baby will need to find an alternate route : that is a C-section, a Caesar or *" Vaginal Bypass"* as the Obs calls it. ☺

The ultrasound begins and I am more confident as to what to expect, so I ask the lady can I take photos etc. She asks me to wait until later.

She applies the lubrication jelly to the belly and the tv screen shows us our baby. I remind the lady that we do not want to know the sex and she tells us that the baby is that big now that we will not see much. It's so true, the baby is crushed up in there and I wonder how the poor little thing is doing. I tell you, I'd cry for months if I had to go through that ☺

The lady starts measuring the head, the black patch in the uterus [which tells her the levels of amniotic fluid in there], she measures the heartbeat, length of baby [crown to rump] and the blood flow from baby to placenta, and alas the placenta's distance from the exit door [cervix].

All went well for us and the news that we had no "Placenta Previa" was all good but I think it dawned on my wife that now the option for natural birth was in the mix. I think silently she got used to the idea that she needed to have a C-section so now all options were back on the table :

- C-section – recovery is longer for the woman but no labour is needed & there's no stress for the baby.

- Natural birth – Painful but recovery is quicker.
- Natural birth with drugs –
  reduces the pain but more expensive &
  comes with the risks if an epidural is
  chosen.

During the ultra sound I asked the lady about the 3D view on the screen, and she flicked it on. At first all you see is brown lumpy clouds, but through the clouds eventually a picture comes through:

There it was: our baby's face.

My first reaction was *"where is it?"*, then I saw the little face. There were the little eyes closed, the little hand and alas one very strange looking nose!

It looked really flat and wide and the nostrils slope down? What do you say? Do you pretend it's all okay and just move on?? There it was my baby looked liked Martin Luther King? : "*They can take your life but will never take your Pride !*" was playing in my head.

I asked my wife what she thought and she also thought the baby's nose looked pressed against glass or something? The poor thing. It's always easier to say things like that about other people's kids, but not your own. My wife and I joked that if the baby got my head and her nose that it would look extremely weird. For now we stopped laughing.

To the right of the picture there was a black patch and apparently that was the leg of the baby? The poor little thing was so squashed in there.

Afterwards I was allowed take the photo of my wife on the bed with all the equipment around and we walked out and paid.

My wife went to empty her bladder after holding in all that water that helps the ultrasound pictures and I was left to pay the boring receptionist. As I paid her $300 for ten minutes work I sarcastically said *"Jaysis, the Ultra sound business is a good one to be in".*

In line with her personality she answered my comment with:

"Well you want the baby to be taken well care of, don't you?"

I sarcastically agreed and we left. Funny that she was answering some other question but I suppose I was saying something else too.
Ultrasounds are a rip off. If Richard Branson wants a new venture for the *'Virgin'* brand then here it is. Virgin Ultrasound's – I love the irony!

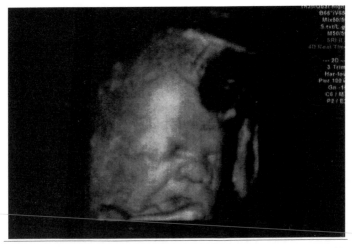

Middle Earth

Week 35/36

Well all's ready now. The bag is packed. The substitute driver is ready and the wife is getting up more often during the night to drink milk or put the heat pack in the microwave. Any day now......

Lots of people keep asking me when the baby is due and the *"It will be soon now"* comments keep coming, and I am forced into having the same conversation with lots of people:

"Yes, Yes soon now"...... "4 weeks or so"....

It's when you utter those words that the reality does click in again. Keep enjoying your sleep and going out as this will change. We've been through this before but it does ring truer & truer as the time moves on. I keep repeating this to myself. It's become a mantra. I know the end is near. That mentality has returned.

The other thing you'll really notice is that you can't drink anymore. Yes that's right, you are on call to drive your lovely wife to the hospital! The Cheek.

There will be social events where you might drink a few more than you should, but you do run a risk. Imagine being the muppet who was plastered for the birth day. Ringing a taxi, slurring, paying for the wet-patch in the back seat, trying to interact with the hospital staff, getting the dagger eyes from them & the wife and all this backed up with a dirty hangover which will over shadow all the experience and happiness of it.

The message then, is stay healthy, stay sober, be ready & enjoy!!!

Week 36+

It's like the baby is already here in some ways. She is washing the baby clothes in soap flakes, you have baby stuff everywhere and not to mention the room that the baby has taken over upstairs. I suppose though if you are not used to the idea after all this journey then you never will be.

> *You don't realise you're going on a holiday until you're on the plane you know? – this is the same feeling so pack your bags!*

The visit with the Obs was a good one. It reconfirmed that we had no fears of "Placenta Previa" and I cleared up a lot of action items that I needed to clarify :

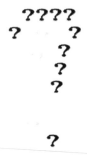

The Final Questions :

Me : On Game day do I ring you on the way to the hospital? :

Obs : " The hospital will ring me straight away but I am happy to give you my mobile anyway".

Me: When it comes to contractions – I only ring Birth Centre when they are 2 – 3 minutes apart?

Obs: "Well you can ring when they are 5 minutes apart, just monitor the regularity of them. If they are regular then you will probably be asked to come in."

Me: If the waters Break?

Obs:"Of course come in"

Me: These Braxton Hicks contractions? How do we know the difference with real ones?

Obs: "These are not painful. Real ones are painful. Also the regularity is not there. Some women do not get them."

Me: Now there is no "Placenta Previa" we will be aiming for a natural birth? What else do we need to decide on now?

"We'll run through all that on the day. We will review things as they go. For such an unpredictable thing it is hard to lock away exact plans".

There you go so no birth plan is needed.

Me: When it comes to drugs, what do we need to know?

Obs: "We'll run through that on the day. The morphine will only last two hours so there is no use taking it early in the labour. If you want to go down that way we would usually recommend an epidural. This can last as long as you want and can even be done for after birth. It's up to you."

Me: What about Gas?

Obs: " This is useless. It will make you a bit dreamy, that's all"

Cool I'll try that.

Obs :"So there are no real considerations to worry about"

Me: Except expense though?

Obs: " No, there will be a specialist there on the day and they will give you the epidural".

That was it. All ready now I think. One last check of the wife's bloodpressure and the position of the baby and we were finished. Until next week's visit: Blood test & vaginal swab ?????

Nooooooooooooooooooooooooooooooooooooooooooo. That word *'swab'* is just wrong.

The Beginning

The Baby Name?

Okay I have my ideas on this one and we have discussed a few names between us. The fact my sister used my name has ruled me out of using that name again, or maybe not? I'll argue for the final shortlist anyway.

There have always been a couple of names that we liked for both sexes. The golden rule has always been to not tell anyone what names we are thinking as they will always try to shape your decision and annoy you.

The thing about the names is you and your wife [and others if you tell them] will immediately think of people you know of or have met throughout your life who had the same or similar name. For example that weird girl you mooched when you were fifteen is not going to make the short list. And you don't need to tell her why - just give the *"No - I just don't like it"* . The less said the better.

The other consideration is the "rhyme trick" – if the names rhyme with something bad the kids in school will destroy the kid – so be sensitive. Although you may not care about this, and good on you Randy Andy.

Anyway there will be a few names you both agree on. We sat down one night and made a short list. My wife had actually read those 'Name' books and read out the ones she liked. We turned the tv off and she rattled off the girls names. Originally she had 33 boys and wait for it: 47 girl's names!

The Beginning

There were some unspellable, unpronounceable ones in there. After sifting through them [be sensitive as her hormones are all over the shop] we rounded them down to 8 boy names & 14 girls!

Names:

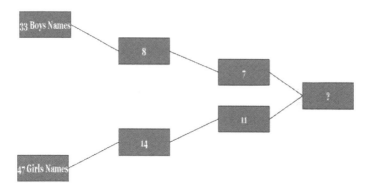

The process is fun actually but just remember to get your opinion in the mix. After a further reading we ended up with 7 boys and 11 girls!

We left it at that and decided to review the names again in a week or so.

Week 37+

Within that time I noticed my wife is starting to get restless and I am wondering is this the *"nesting"* that they all talk about.

Another new behaviour that she went through is *"Droppsey"*. Anything she went to lift all dropped to the floor and I ended up picking up after her. Interestingly she never drops the chocolate milk, chocolate bar, and chocolate ice-cream that she devours every night. Also immune to the *"Droppsey"* are the Indigestion tablets that she consumes by the minute. She texted me the other day and asked me to pick her up a 96 pack ?!? This has got to be a joke. Apparently 16 a day is allowed but I do try and hide the packs as often as I can & I suppose it is keeping her from eating the soap flakes and white chalk.

She has really late showers, she's really restless and she can be knarkey. You wouldn't take her on a fishing trip put it that way.

As we got closer to the 3 week countdown I did notice that this restlessness disappeared. She does get tired early and wakes up very early – just like a young baby I suppose.

The baby has moved down a bit & apparently not touching off her nerves, so her back muscles are not as strained. The requests for massages have lessened but the requests to touch the belly are heightened. This is a nice trade off.

The belly is always out now as she watches tv or is in bed reading those baby books. Sometimes the movement is so obvious it does look like those scenes from the movie *"Alien"*.

All is well. The notion that the baby is big enough to survive and could come out at any time is cool. The other day you could see the belly jump to the rhythm of hiccups and I put my mouth to the belly and told the baby it would be okay. The hiccups stopped ..... for a while. Pretty cool. The legs are definitely at the top and the head and arms toward the exit door. It becomes quite easy to pick what is moving in there.

The Closing Stages:

Emotional, tired, sore back, eating lots of chocolate
and ice cream, over busy on getting the house ready?

If all this sounds like your wife then you are wrong.
This was me.

I found myself experiencing all these things. It was as
if we were identical twins and what she experienced , I
experienced. I didn't even realise it until I was
complaining about my back in work. Someone told me
it was the old *'sympathy pregnancy'* thing!

Sympathy Pregnancy thing ? What the ? Apparently it
is common enough. As soon as I heard about it though
- it did make sense. The other day going to work I was
driving for the first time in ages and I had the stereo
all to myself. I started listening to some old tunes and
as I was screaming/singing along with them, I found
myself getting real emotional. I nearly cried to be
honest with you & I remember asking myself *" where
have you been?"*

Then there's the chocolate and ice cream eating and
the wife has me busy busy with house duties. I think
I'm nesting !

It's funny and I'm not too sure how long it'll last ☺

She goes to bed early always now but if she is
disturbed at all she can't get back to sleep, she says.
Apparently she's been up some nights and just gets
busy doing housework while I'm asleep .. And I

thought it was elves or something cleaning the place while we slept. ☺

The other day the babyshower finally happened and I headed out with the lads.

As mentioned previously, these Babyshowers are not the done thing, where I come from. People buy presents after the birth and not before. Perhaps this springs from an idea that people don't want to give presents until the baby is actually born, healthy and all good. Perhaps based in an old culture that used to experience a lot of baby deaths. Here though, in Australia the culture is younger, the people more optimistic perhaps and the fact the idea came from America, it makes good business to have a gang of women get together and buy baby stuff.

The mother in law and sister helped deck the house out with baby decorations, gathered food and nappies and baby bottles for games. What happened next I do not know as firstly, I left it to the women, and secondly I went down the pub with the lads and got drunk. [I was given the night off being "on call" as the house had plenty of back up – although if the labour started while I was down the pub, things would have been interesting].

Upon my return the place still had a few drunken talking stragglers and loads and loads of baby presents. The "present register" which my wife put together really worked and we received so much essential stuff that we would have had to buy ourselves. This whole baby shower thing is a great idea as you need all the help you can get when it comes to money. I won't ponder on this again but the whole optimistic culture of the babyshower does help bring optimism for the baby's arrival. Get her to have one.

Another Obs Visit:

The next visit to the Obs started with a blood test for the wife, but ended with the Obs having to run for it and go deliver twins.

Annoying at the time, yet that is exactly what you want him to do for you when you make the call.

It's strange now, everywhere I go I am conscious that the baby may come. The phone is constantly in my view but there are still times that I forget it and run the risk that I'll miss the call.

Being our first baby, I am taking the general view of what *"they"* say and running with the notion that the first baby will probably be on time or late. However that did not stop me cancelling a work trip abroad and cancelling any long trips on the road. I want to be within a couple of hour's circumference from the mother to be.

The roller coaster of emotions is full up and down, and the times that I get excited are definitely matched with the times that I am nervous about the whole thing. The change coming makes me nervous. All natural I suppose.

People keep asking me *" Are you excited?"*, and I answer using the analogy that : " it's like a *holiday – I don't realise I'm going on holiday until I'm on the plane – you know"* .... The plane is leaving soon and our bags are packed.

A friend asked me the other day how long was left and I found myself about to say 3 weeks, but I stopped and double checked the calendar on the phone. As I clicked through the weeks, there were only two so I clicked right to count the few days after that. Wow, how did that happen? 2 and half weeks left! Be warned the long wait suddenly fly's in. Bring the phone to the toilet, to the gym and into those meetings. You are officially on call – you are going to be a Dad & really soon !!!!!!!!!!!!!!

The other week, we went through the contents of the hospital bag and we were surprised to find stuff we forgot to pack. We wrote a few things on a big sticker and put it on the bag. My wife finishes work tomorrow and will not have to work again for another 6 months.

The Last Essentials:

The last few things for the bag she can get. I am just revising in my head the essential things I need to know & do:

- Keep phone on at all times – you're on call!

- When things start – keep her calm.

- Help her stretch or walk around or into the bath
  [not if waters have broken]

- Time the contractions

- Remember: they need to be consistent & getting closer to each other

- If they are 4 or 5 minutes apart get ready to go

- If the waters break – GO!

- If you don't know what to do – ring the hospital !!

- Bring the bag & check list before you go

- Let the professionals do their job

That's pretty much it I think. We've talked about going for the natural birth & if she wants the drugs I am to allow it – I'll just work with the advice of the doctor's of course.

I think that covers my role in it, the rest is up to her. Tough job and I will be there to help her. Jaysis lads, we definitely have the easier gig.

Week 38+
Well into last 2 weeks now ....

The other night watching tv, my wife let out a yelp & I thought this is it & it really hit home that the baby could come at any minute. It worked out it was a false

The Beginning

alarm, but I got real panicky cause I really believe the birth would be on time. The panicking really forced me to think about what <u>exactly</u> I had to do. It was time to 'Man-up' for action, so I got to simplifying what it was I had to do. There was no more bullsht - it's time to cut to the chase:

- Ring hospital when sht happens
- Keep her as relaxed as possible
- Bring the bag and grab some food/drink and last minute things while she is 'Relaxing' at home
- Try not to get sick or freak out if waters or mucus stuff comes out!!

Another thing I read that stood out is that I need to make sure that when the contractions are well under way that she does the panting instead of pushing. Why? Cause it will tear! That's a dual investment down there so you don't want your wife to go through pain but you don't want that area to be too messed up as a result either – there are further uses for that later you know what I mean. ☺

Speaking of which – the sex has totally dried up now – zero – nada – nothing!

Two lads in work [who have kids by the way] were slaggn me off saying my balls must be weighing me down etc, etc & saying that it will get worse after the birth. A watch out only lads, I'm going through it now so will let you know. Although I am not too sure if I'll get the green light to talk about this stuff in this book.

If you are reading this now [firstly thank you, and secondly I've either got the green light or have failed to tell her about it.

The Beginning

The Last Week

We have 1 week left now and the time has slowed right down again. Everything and everyone talks about the baby now, my patience is being tested. I just want it to happen and I can only imagine what my wife is thinking. Lately she is getting up at silly times during the night but then gets back into bed by the time I wake up. The fact she is on maternity leave means we have had quite a lot of nights out & I notice sometimes when she talks she looks like she is going to burst into tears of excitement but apparently she feels just normal. It's an appearance that she seems to have - a glow or something. My view is she is overdosing on the hormones.

From time to time she gets impatient and wants it to be all over but mostly she just carries on and is quite excited.

The girlfriends and family keep her occupied and she has had plenty of time spoiling herself on facials and all that other stuff the girls do. Fair play to her she totally deserves it.

I find myself having very long weekends now as I am not drinking and the time seems calm but there is something not right with me and I put that down to nerves. Everything is about this baby now and the baby has not showed up yet. Maybe that's all it is.

The whole difference in lifestyle is an obvious stress but I think the main thing is the anticipation on what to do when things start to happen. It's a rollercoaster, up and down confidence but I think I am okay on what I need to do.

My wife handed me a book the other day with lots of purple page markers hanging out of them. She wants me to read it all so I know what to do when the labour kicks in. I really think there is too much to know sometimes and I think the *'keep it simple'* philosophy is best here. I'm not suggesting I just go and wing it but I think all I can do is be there, keep her calm, give her what she wants and drive her to the hospital. Then the professionals will take over. That's the simplistic version anyway. The anticipation of when is the big thing now. The how is pretty clear. Like a fisherman waiting on a fish but for a very, very long time.

Week 39, 1 day

Today we had potentially our last visit with the Obs.

It was the usual routine, we sat down, he greeted us and asked how things were and whether we had any concerns/questions. My wife explained a pain she has being getting: a sharp pain that *"shoots through ... "* he finished the sentence that she didn't want to and said, *"that shoots through the vagina.."* he went on to clarify that this would be the baby's head hitting off the cervix. I asked again was it those Braxton Hicks contractions and he said *"No"* and clarified that they are non-consistent, near painless contractions.

Then I asked the Obs out straight:

"What do I need to do?" :

He said, *" if the contractions are between 3-5 minutes apart then ring the hospital and start making your*

way in. Or if the waters break then do the same".
That was it.

I wanted to know whether it typically starts with
contractions about half hour apart and they work their
way closer but he clarified with his simple and
conclusive tone that the labour is all uncertain: some
women start a half hour apart and that can last for a
day, while others can start quickly and have baby
within a few hours. Simply put:

**"Nobody knows what to expect so chill out
and wait and see".**

Next we went in and propped my wife up on the same
table/bed thing and jelly on belly and a quick scan of
the baby. This and a quick feel of the belly reveals the
babies position: head down, facing the side and all
normal and on track.

The Obs then measures the belly from vagina to top
and I find myself asking what is the cervix - *" The wall
at the exit"?*

I'm told that is right and he explains that it is 4 inches thick and thins right down at the end and then opens, separates and allows the baby to get out.

The cervix is always a part of the woman's body and is why the girls need to get the swab check thing every few years. Enough said.

Then the blood pressure is measured and the card is filled out by the Obs and he explains that we have a 50% chance of seeing him next week and 50% chance of seeing him earlier. I could not get a grasp on his odds but took his word for it. The message – the inevitable is real close now. To be honest we are both over it at this stage and are looking forward to meeting the baby and seeing what all the fuss is about.

Before we head away my wife asks about the " *Episiotomy".*

Now this is a word that should send chills down anyone and is something a mate told me to google a while back. I didn't but found out that it is when the doctors have to cut the skin between the vagina and the anus to allow more room for the baby to get out. OUCH!

To be honest the Obs was brilliant in explaining it and told us the incision [doesn't sound as bad that way] is done sideways so that there is no tear between the vagina and the anus. Those 3 words : Vagina, Tear & Anus did send shivers through me but I was pleasantly surprised to see how calm my wife was about this whole subject [excuse the bum, I mean pun].

The Obs explained that the baby's head is bone and is

therefore going to win the battle out the exit door made of skin. It is only possible to tell whether tearing is going to be a problem at the late stage. The Obs will make a call at that stage. He explained that if it is thought that tearing is possible then the Episio is better than risking the tearing, which will go vertical toward the anus and be harder to repair than a horizontal incision.

At this late stage the touching and talking of vagina by the Obs is second nature. Any strangeness has disappeared

I'm realising as I write this that I need to stop writing about this subject as it is probably making you sick but the reality at this late stage is that you do get very used to all this gorey and vagina talk. The other thing I noticed after the Obs meeting is that I was asking loads more questions than my wife and infact I am stressing/worried potentially more than she is. So there you go – this is not easy for the boys either eh. Definitely a team effort and the team are going to get a new member.

The two hurdles that new team member have to go through are:

1. The head must get through the narrowest part of the pelvis. If it can't then a c-section is the way out.

2. If the head gets through the narrowest pelvis part, then c section is out of the way & the only concern is will the head be too big on the way out. This will answer whether an Episio is needed or not.

The odds of which I have no idea of, so in the name of optimism let's say the chances that Episio rears his head is very, very rare. There - that feels a bit better!

So with all that put on the table we left potentially our last meeting with the simple strategy on when to head for the hospital and the understanding as to what decisions we need to make or may need to make.

More confident now we left with the 50/50 chance of our next meeting being Game Day!

It's funny at the beginning, I used to worry if my wife sneezed as I thought it may freak the small jelly bean / baby out inside. All this Episo/ vaginal talk leave all that in its wake.

Everything was all about how to best relax her during the labour. I got to thinking – I was told the average number of contractions are 187, if I need to help relax her through all of that then it's me who'll need some help too. I've got to get the energy drinks in & battle through it with sugar.

Week 39, 2 days :
4.43 am .....

Okay I'm very tired. At 4.43 am the wife woke me up sitting on my side of the bed and said *" I think the waters have broken?"* and she calmly smiled at me.

I of course was still half asleep and there is something about the early hours of the morning that are so calm.

I asked her what happened & she explained that she woke to go to the toilet and on the way there were drips, then she went to the toilet and there were more drips on the way back to bed. Then she lay there with tissue and it was drenched and was a pinkish colour apparently. She went downstairs to chill and then decided to wake me with the smile.

My initial reaction was that this was not it as I am expecting the whole contraction thing and the pain etc, but there was none of that. I really tried to remember what I had read but could not. It may have been the morning brain or just the man brain but I forgot what I had read. I pulled out the hospital booklet and read the signs of labour bit and it referred to the "show'" of mucus so I thought it would be that. In my mind the contractions should happen first right?

Anyway I followed the golden rule – if in doubt just call. I rang the hospital from bed and a bloke answered. I told him I thought my wife maybe going into labour and he asked me my name and how long we were pregnant. I struggled with both answers as I didn't know if she had her maiden name registered and the second answer I looked for clarification that we were 39 weeks or so pregnant. After that I realised I was having a shocker so I needed to wake up, stand up and get busy taking control.

The bloke on the other end then put us through to a midwife and she was to talk with my wife so I handed over the phone. I was in control of that.

I could hear the lady ask what had happened, whether it was our first baby and to my surprise asked her to come in for a check-up.

Calmly, and in tune with the vibe of 5 am we got ready to go. I grabbed the bags, ipod doc, books, energy drinks and off we went.

Remembering to use the car with the baby seat in it we drove to the hospital. There were a few people walking but most were asleep. It felt like a perfect day to bring a baby into the world.

My wife was very calm. I parked up and we went in.

The guy who had answered the phone was at reception and a cleaner rocked up to the counter with his morning tea. My wife was asked to sign all these papers and we had to make sure we didn't sign the wrong details. For example one form was stating we agreed to pay the excess for a single room but we weren't properly covered so we had asked before to change this. Anyway she filled in the paperwork and he pressed a button which shot open the corridor doors into the labour ward.

We approached another reception with 5 women and one man behind it talking. They were a lot friendlier than the paper pusher at the first desk and we were introduced to our mid-wife: Glen. Isn't he a mid-husband?

Anyway he was quite cool. We walked to a room. My wife lay down and then needed to go to the toilet again. Glen gave her some giant pads to use and a swab kit to diy. In she went while me and Glen shared some small talk and I discovered he was finishing in an hour and that it had been a quiet night.

The Beginning

My wife returned, lay down and was hooked up to this machine. Two straps went around her back and belly and Glen fitted two grey sensor type discs to the belly area. One was located to listen out for the baby's heart beat and the other was centered.

This was linked to a rather old fashioned looking machine that had two digital numbers flashing and a scroll of paper that had two pens that swivelled based on the baby's heart beat and the contractions. The pens swivelled up and down and drew a graph on the paper.

Glen then explained that we didn't want to see a flat line, [No sht Glenie boy] and wanted the heart beat to be between 110 and 160. He explained that there is an old wives tale that states the lower the heart beat the chances are it is a boy. Our baby was beating around the 120 mark. Our feelings that it is a boy just increased again with that tale.

The second digital displayed a number that was to act as a bench mark from which contractions can be measured. This monitoring had to go for at least two sheets of paper or ten minutes. To our surprise there were readings of tightening and contractions but my wife could not feel them. We were not near labour yet.

Glen pointed out that her belly was still quite loose and that when in labour, the belly tightens right up. He tested the blood pressure and temperature and then we were released to go home and return again later in the day between 2 and 2.30. As we left, Glen told us that there was a 90% chance that the baby would arrive within 24 hours of the *'membrane rupturing'*.

I had been skeptical as to whether the water had broken up to that point as I would have expected a large volume of water. Anyway we were free to go. I was happy to see I did not get a parking fine and so we drove home, bought bread, made a b.l.t., texted the boss and got down to resting. The calm before the storm I feel.

We went back to sleep soon after we got back. She went asleep on the couch and only woke up when her feet fell off the edge. We moved up to the bed and conked out. Of course she woke first and I rested up. She came back to sleep just before we had to go back for another appointment and off we went again: hospital bag, back into the car, turn left out of the driveway and head for the hospital. We brought everything at this stage as who knows when the whole thing will kick off.

Week 39, 3 days :

We had to go to a different part of the hospital this time and we eventually found our way through the labyrinth of hospital corridors. I swear it is like 'Alice in Wonderland' when looking for places: there is activity going on in many rooms, around corners, there are voices and the occasional passer by helps by pointing us in the right direction.

This time we had a female midwife, an older lady called Helen. She was made for the job, she had a natural , gentle character and a real interest in the whole baby process. Just a genuine feel about her that all she wanted to do was help.

Into a room we went and it was much of the same: the wife onto a fold back chair, strapped in and the lady placed the two discs on the belly and started to track the baby's heart beat & the number of mild contractions. This time though the baby was sleeping and it was hard for the lady to get a good read on the heart. She had to get at least 10 minutes of a good awake read so she could give it to a doctor to sign off and then we could go.

Because of this, we were longer than last time but it was all good. You do feel safe in there but the rooms can start to move in on you. It is good to get out. The midwife also had to check the giant maternity pad in my wife's knickers and so my wife had to pull it down to show her. The lady's reaction was not that positive in my view, so off she went to get a second opinion. Apparently they want to see a pinkish clear colour so maybe there was something different. Needless to say I did not volunteer to look at this, I just sat where I was told and we waited for another midwife to enter. She was funny, she came in and said *"okay where's the pad?"*.. and upon realising it was still on my wife she said *" Okay drop your Dacks"*.

We all laughed and the awkwardness was slapped out of the room. Her opinion was enough to lay the older midwife's concerns to rest.

We were free to go, well after the nurse went off to ring our Obs and tell him the latest. She came back and booked us in for another check-up the following day.

Off we went with new instructions in hand. There is this A4 sheet of paper that they gave us and it details what we are to monitor:

1. *the colour of the flow from the exit door [
    should be pinkish or clear, green, brown or a
    deep yellow may mean the baby is distressed].*
2. *The wife's temperature every 4-6 hours while
    awake, [making   sure it is < or = to 37.2
    degrees Celsius].*
3. *The baby's movements – as often as before.*

If any of the above are not as they should be then ring
the hospital.

At home that night it kind of feels like a holiday as
neither of us are working now and we just ordered
food in and got lots of dvd's.

We slept like babies that night and I was only woken
up by the wife going to the toilet or getting up for her
usual food or mid sleep stretching. Her back gets so
sore that she can't stay in one place for as long as we
can.

Week 39, 4 days :

This day we woke up, followed the routine to the car,
the hospital and the room. We had the same *"drop
your Dacks"* midwife as the day before and the same
procedure and tests.

We had a long time in the room on our own this time
and the stereo sound of the baby's heart beat from the
not-so-primitive machine that tracked everything was
amazing. It sounds so calming and would send you to
sleep.

Everything was normal and we were told we would be all systems go for the Inducing tomorrow at 8 am! My wife was a bit reluctant about this now and would prefer to wait another day to see if she can go naturally. The midwife rang the Obs and she explained that the lack of staffing over the weekend, the fact the Obs was on the labour ward all day & that the increased risk of infection all lead to the argument for the Inducing to kick off tomorrow Friday morning at 8 am!

That was that then. We would meet our baby tomorrow!

During all of this, the family, close friends & even boss are constantly texting and ringing to get an update. It did feel a little like the announcement of the pregnancy when we told people about the *" breaking of the waters".*

I told the boss, family and A-team friends in that order. The calls and texts are constant this time round and they can get annoying. My advice is to manage everyone's expectations and just tell them you will keep them informed when/if things change.

I am starting to feel that the family may all rush to the hospital when I tell them we are going into labour so I have had to retell all of them that I don't want to see them until I call them.

Week 39, 5 days :
Bringing on the Labour

Today though we met the mother-in-law after the appointment and had lunch and I really wanted to get my wife to walk, to help bring on the labour.

There is lots of random advice floating around about this:

> - Have sex *[we can't though as the waters have broken]*
> - Eat spicey food   *[?]*
> - Lots of walking/moving *[but you want to make sure she rests so she has energy for the labour]*
> - Gin and tonic *[this came from my socially-alcoholic sister so not sure how true that one is]* ☺

When we got home after a walk in the mall, lunch and a walk in the park we started to do some DIY around the place. The free time and the knowledge that I won't have anytime after the birth, all got me into busy mode. Upon reflection though : perhaps I was nesting? I thought this at the time and purposely got my wife involved again, to try and get her busy to help bring on the labour. Part of me wants it all to be natural, but I suppose you have to trust the medics on this one. All will be well. It's time for more DVD's now. My wife has had a few small yelps and explained that there *"maybe something going on"*. The volume and intensity that I expect is not there though so I remain calm. The small yelps are coupled with a real rise in temperature. A mini contraction perhaps?

Time will tell. Time to chill and see what happens. I'll see you on the flip side!

The Beginning

Week 39, 6 days :
The Contractions

Well at the stroke of midnight the contractions started. Before that we had a normal night of TV and food and I talked to the baby and told it to come out soon. I made a point of talking into the belly from a lower position so as to encourage it to make its way.

When the contractions started – I thought the baby started to listen. *'Good boy'* I thought & reminded myself not to be sexist and also thought *'Good girl'*.

Once started, my wife could not lay down properly and had to breathe heavily : the stuff you expect and see in the movies. She was actually happy as she now knew what the feeling was really like. However I knew that these were mild ones but didn't point that out.

They tended to last nearly 45 seconds and were sporadic. I remembered to time them and eventually got used to the idea that I needed to time from the start of one contraction to the start of another. I initially thought it would be from the end of one to the start of another but hey they know best?

I was using the 'lap time' on the phone so the battery was running out big time as the contractions started to roll on in.

They started to last between 45 seconds and 1 minute and were about 8 – 10 minutes apart. This went on for a really quick 2 hours or so. They were still relatively mild and I just kept being positive to my wife and told her that the baby was coming naturally and all was well.

The crazy thing about the contractions is the straight back to normal part after they are finished. We had our lap top fired up watching doco's and so went straight back into watching them after each contraction. They seem to peak in the middle and fall toward the end. Therefore a 60 second one is starting to chill out after 30 seconds.

After a while the contractions started every two to three minutes and it took about ten in a row before I rang the hospital. The lady figured out that the fact we were happy to stay home and my wife was not screaming for drugs that we were still not in full labour. We were told to stay put and we did.

There were moments there when I thought that the sudden frequency of contractions was so quick that I started to imagine a scenario where **I had to deliver the baby.**

After that day dream though we lay down to bed watching a movie and we slept on the couch. There were more contractions but less often. All I did was tell her she would be alright and at the half way mark to start to go back asleep. This worked and we both got some rest, moved up to bed and tried again. Sure enough there were more contractions but after talking to the hospital again we were both confident that this was all early days. We managed to both sleep and after a while [while I conked out] the contractions slept too. We woke up in the morning and were due in hospital for an 8 o'clock inducing.

The Beginning

I rang the Obs as my wife was worried and told him the story. He told us to monitor things from home and said if no contractions happened again or if regular 60 second ones started, that lasted 3-5 mins, to come in. We had the former and went into hospital for 11 to do a standard check-up again.

We knew though as we left home this time that we would return as a family of 3. That is quite a cool thought. The check up wasn't so cool and was more of the same.

Eventually the Obs showed up and immediately started to tell us that the pro's of inducing were starting to outweigh the cons as the level's of bacteria in the belly would start to rise as the days had passed since the waters broke. We went along with this and were told we could go out to have lunch and then come back for the inducing.

Game Day
Week 40 exactly :

Off we went then. Texted all the clan so they were aware and we headed for this really snug looking café that we drove past many times on our way to the hospital.

It's very surreal doing this. You leave the hospital

intact and you know this is the last chance saloon: the last lunch as a twosome, the last normal couple time before the birth, the calm before the storm, the chicken before the egg - it was mad knowing that everyone was just getting on with their day, while we were heading back into hospital to experience one of the maddest things anyone can experience. Surreal, normal, weird, frightening & cool all mixed together. Walk on.

Today after lunch on the way to the hospital we stopped at a petrol station to get some snacks etc. My wife turned around and looked straight at me and said that she was *"so happy to go through this with me."*

It made me feel so emotional and happy. The only thing was we were at the automatic door of a petrol station so I couldn't get too into it when the doors swung open and the dude behind the counter is looking. All in all though the emotional part was kicking in.

On the way to the hospital it kind of felt like when we were going to do a bungy jump. You are volunteering for something risky but with high chance of a happy ending.

When we got to the hospital we got a good parking spot and I carried all the bags in: the main bag & a food bag. Then we found out that wife cannot eat after being induced. That would make the whole thing a bit messy later on. [All the chocolate, snacks and energy drinks are all mine now.] ☺

We walked into the hospital and gave the nod to the lady at reception and walked to our room number 9, to settle in.

The wait is long before someone comes in to see to us. Eventually a mid wife comes in and introduces herself. Name tags go on the wife's wrist. The midwife examines the exit door to see if it's open. She hands me this long off yellow coloured rod and asks me to hold onto it. At the end of the rod is a small hook - this will be used to break the waters if the membrane inside has not been broken.

It was a shock that I had to hold this. There were a lot more shocks on the way and I knew it.

The inducing fluid was hooked up to my wife through a drip and the lady insisted on chatting for ages and explaining the dosage theories and then some general chit chat. I was in no mood for this though - we had checked into this room 9 and hooked up our laptop and had movies on and it really seemed like it was 'room service' or a chambermaid staying too long in our strange looking hotel room.

The inducing fluid would take a while so my priority was to chill out with the wife and try and rest before the Game really started.

Time will be a marathon. I have tried to keep the relaxing aids to a minimum like you would 'save your lives' in a computer game or in 'who wants to be a millionaire' but they have all nearly run out: we've tried bending over bed, the music is on, the oil is burning and I've tried to massage her. The ball is out and she is sitting on it.

Time seems to past so fast in here. The clock ticks

loud and ticks fast. The dosage goes up in 15 ml increments and after 5 hours we are in full swing. The midwife comes in every 30 mins to increase the dosage – it feels at the moment that she is coming in every 5 minutes. That's all good though, time is going fast - let's get this over with ! Each time she increases the dose of the hormone, syntocinon, which is a fabricated version of oxitocin that the body normally produces.

Each time the midwife is in, I am so tired that I am trying not to catch her eye as she talks. I have pegged her as a "Chatter-box" and she will not shut up if you show the slightest bit of interest. My wife of course is hanging on every word. I would too if roles were reversed.

It's funny, I discovered through this process that it takes a while for me to warm to someone but I am slowly getting used to her and she is growing on me.

I hadn't realised that my wife cannot eat anything and as well as that, the only drinks she can have are clear liquids : the safe bet is water or ice or hot water. She's spoilt for choice. ☺

The nature music worked for a while, the oil burning helps but I can't even smell it now. She panicked a bit about one of the oils running out so I told her I'd ask her sister to get some more.

Labour

The contractions really kicked in then. Regular as clockwork every 3 minutes or less and they got more painful. All this is expected of course but the reality is a different kettle of fish:

I tried massaging her, tried the different positions on the bed and standing up. God love her she feels like she needs to go to the toilet after each one and the fact she is on this induction drip means we have to unplug it and walk with a metal stand to the toilet. The heat pack came in handy for 1 or 2 contractions, again the affect or novelty did not last long.

The bouncing ball worked for a while and I held her hips and helped her move around when the contractions started.

Basically all these aids only worked for a few contractions with my wife - what a pain in the arse - time for Drugs !!

At this stage you are full time at work and the mid wife is in and out on her half hour visits to monitor things. She wants to see the contractions and pain start and she wants to quickly measure the babies heart beat etc. All is well.

The midwife did need to check the dilation of the cervix at one point and she got my wife into position and, again, asked me to hold this long, plastic rod with a small hook on the end of it. It would be used to pierce the water membrane if she found it. Anyway she went in there with her fingers during a contraction and told us we were 1 cm dilated and could feel the baby's head. She could not find the membrane to burst so I was off the hook, so to speak. My wife though, was not as you need to be 10 cm to get near birth – a long way to go.

The other thing about being induced means the wife cannot use the nice bath or shower that we have next to us. That would have been great but who knows how many contractions it would have worked for before she got bored again.

The ice worked for one or two as well, but eventually, the mention of drugs started to creep in. We had told the Obs that we were open to using them if the need arose and it arose.

Starting at 4 pm, the inducing started off the contractions 4 or 5 hours later and the drugs were a real option after all the other stuff didn't work. The visualisation thing did not wash with my wife but I did use the 'going up a hill' image to help her realise when the contraction had hit its peak and was descending down hill.

The midwife, Pam, was full on with the sales pitch for morphine and this raised alarm bells with me as she seemed really for it. Not sure why but the thoughts that she might be on a morphine bonus did creep in. Anyway we managed to encourage the idea of gas first and that worked a treat. The tube was connected up and away she went. At each contraction she sucked in. Deep inhaling and exhaling while the pain was felt and the short-term buzz made you feel kind of stoned or giddy, high. How do I know it so well? Because I gave it a whirl a few times and my wife and I had a bit of a laugh. All when the midwife was not there of course. This was great and necessary for a good hour or two and we had heard that this is all some women need. At this stage the midwife Pam was finishing up her shift and we were to be introduced to our new mid wife who was on the night shift & probably the lady who would be there for the birth.

In the mean time, the Obs came in for a brief minute, said hello and basically saw that my wife was in pain but knew it was still early and off he went. My wife joked *"Chi-Ching"* $ 500 dollars for that! We laughed. Her personality was hilarious with this gas stuff.

Eventually these contractions were crazy painful and my wife was in real stress. She grabbed me really tightly with the hand she could use [as the other had the drip in it] and I tried to relax her but it was not working. The upgrade for an epidural was on the cards.

The second examination was due at midnight [four hours after the first one] and I tried to get her to relax after that on the gas. The Obs did pop his head in again and this time in his surgical gear . He was busy, busy and it is great to see a familiar face through all of this. We asked him again about the drug options and he was of the opinion that an epidural was the go at this early stage. In Obs we trust, so it did not take my wife long to decide. The new midwife, Priscilla, was on board now. She was a really well spoken English lady who was also an "OH&S officer" and she was not too fond of my laptop cord near the bed. I took an immediate disliking to her, but as I expected, she grew on me. I ordered one serve of epidural and we were told that the dude would come in and do it after he finished with another patient.

This meant a very slow half hour/hour full of painful contractions for me and my wife to tackle. She was in so much pain now and the breaks were for only 2/3 mins that I and she became anxious so I went out to disturb the midwife's tea break and urge the dude to get in and sort it all out.

Eventually after one last trip to the toilet we were introduced to Simon and his needles. He talked up the risks:

-    1 in 100 get headaches for weeks
-    1 in 25 it doesn't work on [they just try another injection in a different part of the back]
-    1 in 2 million get paralysed

After that , we all agreed the odds were okay and we sat my wife up. I had to tackle her from the front as she was propped over a pillow. He had to wait while contractions finished and then inject my wife first with a local anaesthetic and then the epidural. God love her, in the pain break from the contractions she had to endure this. After keeping her arms relaxed down and to the front he did his bit and the midwife hooked my wife up to a urine bag so all was set. It took 30 or so minutes to kick in but after ten the affect was lessening the pain already. My wife became much more talkative and we got the life story from our midwife and Stuart's opinion on the labour issues of women in Africa. Which was a real fascination for my wife at this point. She was talkative like she would be when she was drunk, so this stuff had some pretty strong affect. She became hungry, cold and shivery now. All this due to the body's reaction to the nerve that tells the brain about pain, heat and cold, being numb. The hunger because she was hungry.

The mood and time got relaxed then. The midwife did her tests and monitors things still while Stuart's work was done. My wife has a slight pain sometimes in one little area and she has a green button for self dosage. The natural music and oils were great now and she slept.

Just after I wrote the line above, the midwife and Obs came in. Things were about to change.

The Home Straight:

First the midwife Priscilla was in and had carried out the second inspection. The cervix was still only at 1 cm. She could see the membrane and decided to get me involved. Again I had to hold this yellow/brown plastic rod with the small hook on its end and pass it to her when she was ready. My wife could not feel a thing at this point so the midwife had fingers in there and was talking to her like we were chill'n out at a café.

The next thing, I was asked to hand the rod over and with a skirmish and look of *"argghh"*, she had busted the membranes and now the waters were 100% broken. It was interesting to note that no matter how many times the midwife had done this, the sight still was uncomfortable for her. She did well to hide it though, and the wife never noticed. I only noticed as I was looking at her and not down there. Anything but. With that, the midwife cleaned it all up and with her fingers told us the cervix was now at 2 cm. Double now already. But I knew this was not good. We needed to be at ten cm. At this stage I just wanted it to happen.

The Obs came in, he sat down and looked at the results spitting out from the machine monitoring the contractions/ heartbeat etc and talking loudly he said:

 "*How are things?, How we feeling*" - intentionally to wake my wife up and it worked.

She dreamily /druggily looked up and he sat there with a chair backwards toward him and summoned us to an update.

He went on to explain:

That after each contraction the baby's heartbeat was going down. Coupled with that, the cervix was still only 2 cm dilated. Therefore it could take another 10 hours for things to happen naturally. Also given the fact that the waters had broken two / three days prior the risk of infection was higher. All up it lead to one conclusion:

"*Let's get the baby out of there*". C-section.

The staff [including two new faces] started working at a really fast pace. Hectic in fact. This got me paniced. I tried not to show it on my face, yet I noticed I was standing back alone and away from my wife while they wheeled in another bed and this bed sized plastic sheet. Realising this I tried to cheer up and move toward my wife but I also didn't want to get in the way.

20 Minutes:

Once the Obs told us what was happening I asked him *"so will the c-section be in 5 minutes, ten or an hour??"* He answered *"in about twenty minutes."* ..

The silent realisation hit us : we would see/have/meet our baby in 20 minutes!

Scrubs were left for me to wear, I was told to pack up all our belongings and doors flung open with the new staff and the sound of business all around. Rush hour had started.

The scrubs on, and photo taken while the midwife & new staff were outside for a minute we realised this was it. My wife was still in a vacuum of tiredness, drugs and awe. I had all this except no drugs. The gas did look tempting but what if the midwife was to come in - I'd look like a right eejit.

These new staff members used a bedsized plastic sheet as an aid to help slide my wife onto the new bed with wheels. She had to take her clothes off and put on scrubs and then they slide her onto a new bed. All this was carried out fast and furious which caused me to panic. There was little communication to us and the pace of things occurring was off the radar. I was totally thrown into a panic but tried to keep a straight face. Inside and in hindsight I hated the new staff member lady who was an older lady with a strong

personality but who, in my view, lacked the calming affect that me and the wife needed at that moment. Granted there was a need for haste but I felt she could have managed our emotions and her speedy, go-go attitude a bit better. Nonetheless, I was told I would be coming back to the room to pick all the stuff up after the birth and off we went : An entourage minus bags down corridors to have a baby.

On the way we met Stuart, the epidural guy, and he asked how she was feeling, the staff chit-chatted that this was the 3rd one tonight and I kept looking at the wife and my heart was racing.

The Birth

I am sitting here as a father. When I first laid eyes on the baby I was in shock. You don't know what to feel. We were rushed along so quickly that it was all so fast. I was stressing big time. The first thing I noticed was that the face was the same as in the 3d scan, but beautiful. The belly slid up and I see the cord with a whitish end to it. We were so in shock but so so so so happy.

I got to hold the baby and cut the cord bit and even held the baby in my arms in a room on my own – amazing, surreal.

Exhausted now – cannot believe it . Feeling of awe still. It's quiet now. How do I hold baby?

I have never, ever experienced or felt anything like this ever. To describe it in words does not do it justice. It's a boom-time rollercoaster of emotions. You feel lost, afraid, happy & high all at the same time. There were moments in there where I was freak'n out on the inside and all I could do was pray that all would be okay. The staff get busy and have no time to manage your emotions now. Shut-up and let them work is the idea. I remember being in a vacuum at one stage and all around me was panic and bustling bees at work. I was afraid and remember thinking that if anything was to go wrong here that my world would be over. I worried for my wife the most and of course for the baby. The worry came from the situation, the staff's urgency and the lack of communication. I surpressed this worry as much as I could but it must have been written all over my face and right smack in the middle of my shuffling body

The Beginning

language.

I tried to settle my wife and say positive things to her to reassure her. I tried, just like I'll try to explain the feelings through what exactly happened:

Like I said earlier, the Obs and midwife had explained that the heart rate of the baby was going down after each contraction. He further explained that the dilation was still way off the necessary 10 cm. Coupled with the risk of infection, the best foot forward was to get the baby out of there. And fast.

As soon as we nodded in agreement then everything changed. From calm to crazy. It was as if I was pushed from behind, into the entrance of the wildest water slide in the world and I didn't know how long it would last or what was at the end.

These new staff came in and my wife was slid onto a new bed with wheels to transport her to the anaesthetic room to get ready for the C-section.

New staff, new pace and new vibe left me in an unknown place that I was not comfortable in. My wife was tired, drugged and fixated on the staff. I was in my own zone and all I could think was - slow down, relax , all is good. I was the one panicing. The staff had game faces on and perhaps this was all normal for them but they did not look relaxed or express any sort of normality. I tried to get eye contact with a few of them but there was no reception. All this lent itself to convincing me that there was something wrong, something up and something strange. 'Help', I thought but to keep face and keep my wife relaxed and free of my panic - I shut the hell up. Inside I was screaming. I was in labour.

You've heard of man flu - this was man labour.

Off we went down the corridors, met anaesthetic Stuart and our destination was the anaesthetic room. There was ice put on her belly, on both sides and then staff, (new fast people, Stuart, no Obs & midwife Priscilla) all tried to chit chat about '*this was the third of the night'* and it just seemed awkward or strange. My wife was doped and on we went.

We turned left toward another corridor and the door first on the immediate left was the anaesthetic room. As we walked in, the Obs was there, another guy in scrubs and another lady. They continued on and pushed the wife through another swinging two door and I was hurriedly asked to stay where I was. *' What the fk?'.*

A chair was slid to me and I sat on it. As I am seated on this chair and trying to see where they have taken my wife - I noticed I was too low to see through the two slender glass partitions on each door and so I stood up. Not a mention of what was going on, I was in full panic mode now and the conspiracy theory kicked in that *" they don't want me to see what is goin on ? why give me a seat that is so low ?? what is happening - Is everything alright? Arghhhhh !!!, I swear if anything goes wrong, "* and so on.

I stood up in this little room that I was in and peaked through the window and could see the staff working away on my wife. I thought this was it, I am not allowed to be beside her for the birth, something must

The Beginning

be wrong ??? I paced around and on the spot, looked at all the medical supplies on the shelves - this was mad.

I could see through the door window when I stood up and could see an operation going on. This time though it was not a medical soap opera or a movie - it was my wife and my baby in there.

After, what seemed a life time, I was allowed in.

The Obs and two new staff members were down at the exit door end and Stuart, the anaesthetic guy, was up top. The mid wife was not around. There was a blue sheet below my wife's chest which spread out and separated top from bottom.

" Jesus - why didn't you tell me?, " I thought as I went toward my wife and held her hand as the blue sheet partition blocked her view of the Obs and the exit door. I grasped her hand and she seemed still drowsy but needed me to ensure her all would be well. I was so relieved to be in there at this stage and only wished one of the staff had managed my expectations as I may have not paniced as much.

Right there at that moment, I relaxed and kept all panics and negative thoughts at bay. I looked around at staff members and they declined my eye contact but I was getting used to that. I grasped my wife's hand and reminded the Obs I did not want to know the sex of the baby.

Stuart the anesethist and Obs asked the wife if she could feel him *'tugging'* down there and she said *"a little"*. Apparently she can feel a little bit but the nerves that trigger pain are switched off. All systems were go. The Obs started doing all he was paid so much money to do. We were blinded by the situation and by the blue sheet partition.

At that moment, time stopped. All I wanted was to hear the cry. Something to tell us life had entered the world. Life had endured. My wife grasped my hand so hard and was crying now. I tried so hard to stay positive inside and out and ushered to her that all will be fine.

I think I prayed to every God & every person at that time. This was the single most important event ever, all your energy & all your wishes are used up right here and right now.

Trade everything in, it's time.

You could hear the Obs at work, and envisioned the instruments getting in there and looking for baby. I looked around again and all the staff were down to business. Time was eternal and eventually something broke the silence:

I don't remember the order in which this happened but it was either the Obs saying *"alright we don't know the sex yet"* or the crying of the baby. But either way I stood up and looked over the blue sheet and there was the baby. Clean, the spitting image of the ultrasound picture and still unsexed. The relief, the feeling, the vacuum, the reality, the baby was unbelieeeeeeeeeeeeeeeeevable!

Try and picture it, a slow motion visual of a blue sheet in front of you. Your heart is racing. Pan up and look over the sheet. Behind it you see, for the first time, your child, your kid, your flesh and blood, your baby. The whole world stopped. There is no volume. Somebody has pressed mute. Maybe it was God.

Whoever it was, I knew I was looking at an angel. The obstetrician must have been holding its wings. Volume comes back. Mute is off. The angel cries. The angel sings.

Standing up, the Obs was holding the baby under its arms, holding it out the exit door he had to create & then he lifted our baby further into the world. Upward he lifted our baby and my eyes were the only ones most interested in seeing what lay below the baby's waist line and above my wife's waist line.

My wife lay blind behind the blue sheet and a baby entered the world - below its waist line I saw swollen girly bits. There was no willy. In absolute happiness, absolute joy & absolute amazement I exclaimed:

" It's a Girl " !

Exhausted Euphoria

That was it. The crying volume came back on. It seemed the vacuum I was in was broken. I was so excited, I talked in high pitch and repeated " *It's a girl, it's a girl* ".

I remember the cry, the little tongue coming out and the tingly feeling of the unknown. This is, single handedly, the greatest event & experience ever. Hard to explain and in a way hard to experience but the outcome is fabulous, that's it, it's fabulous!

At this stage my wife, the missus, *'Mammy'*, still had not layed eyes on the little angel. The baby was wiped and taken to a table-type thing beyond the bed by two women and I was asked to cut the cord. Well technically anyway. [only shorter as the cord had to be cut by the Obs: during a C-section no-one is allowed near the exit door - for obvious reasons]. Still squealing with joy I exclaimed *"it's a girl, ohh a little girl, ohhh she's soo beautiful baby"*.

The baby was then carried over beyond the blue sheet and to Mammy. She was placed almost on my wife's head and there it was - the first time mother & daughter lay eyes on each other. Both exhausted, both beautiful - we were a family now.

The name tags were put onto baby and mother while all this was going on. As well as that, the Obs was busy closing up the exit door beyond the blue sheet. Thanks to drugs, my wife could not feel a thing. With baby by her neck and chest, the only thing she could feel was the euphoria of meeting her little baby. They had shared bodies for a while so this was special for them.

Soon then, it was time for all of us to leave and let the professionals look after Mammy.

Still in awe, and voice only starting to sound normal pitch, I left my wife & walked with the midwife back to room 9 where it all began.

Our mission was to get the bags and more importantly measure & weigh the baby. Our baby girl was wrapped in a towel like hospital thing and looked so cute. She was placed on this clear plastic, bath tub shape trolley and underneath were some clothes, and the placenta in a bag. This they check out later to make sure it is all there so nothing has been left inside.

The excitement you feel is beyond anything: exhausted but wide awake, you see but you don't believe, surreal, stressed nicely & definitely confused yet clear about something.

As we walked back, the conversations with the midwife were energy filled and similar to what my wife was talking about during the labour while the epidural was kicking in. I was telling her how amazing the whole thing is and I tried to share my joy with her, and in fairness she did entertain me politely, but it was clear I was the one experiencing this for the first time and not her. It was old hat for her. We walked down corridors we had done before the birth and this time there was someone new with us.

My little daughter, Acacia, was wrapped so tight in a blue/pink speckled hospital towel type blanket and she cried sometimes.

Walking back into the labour ward, there was no reaction by staff [there's no novelty anymore for them, they try to give you the reaction you want but it is all routine for them]. This is the greatest moment of my life and to these guys it's just another baby. Kind of felt like when doing a surf lesson and the very time you nail your first wave and look for appreciation or encouragement, the bloody instructor is day dreaming - Habituation's a bitch. ☺

As we got back to the room where the bags were and the whole labour had started the midwife was soon to say goodbye, so I asked for a photo and ironically she held up the placenta in her hand and posed. That was weird, and what's weirder still is I have that photo today!

[By the way - some people keep the Placenta, some for souvenir, some to keep as a blood back-up if needed for the baby in an unforeseen near future event - another cost, another decision - we let them dispose of it].

I was back in room 9 where it all began for us and it was just me and baby while the midwife went off to get whatever she needed to get. This was sooo surreal. I looked down at my little daughter and remembered that it was important for the baby to get skin to skin contact. In my own world with my little daughter I whipped my top off and loosened the blanket around her and held her into me. Beautiful you may say - but no. Baby did not agree. She went hysterical. In paranoia I rushed her back down to her blanket, scrabbled my top back on and with humility, tried to cover my baby in the warm blanket again.

Still no sign of the midwife or anyone at all, I spent what seemed a lifetime with this new little person and it was fantastic. I kept looking at her. This little person was half created by me. I am a Dad!?! I am this baby's Father !?! I keep looking at her. She is so fattened up, and so small. She has a full head of hair and yes that Martin Luther King nose is there but not so flat and big in real life.

She's been squashed up in there and now she's free. We're all free now. Exhausted euphoria. Day dream. She cries and it's soft and new. Her tongue does come out looking for something that I can't provide. Her eyes don't really open. I feel helpless when she cries, happy when she's asleep and so excited to tell the family, so excited to sleep and so excited to start this whole stage. Tired too but so excited.

The midwife did come back eventually and she measured my baby. 50 cm long and 3.546 kilos.

Then she brought up a further question which I wasn't prepared for: the vitamin k injection?

She gave me the spiel and as I hadn't discussed this with the wife, I just asked *"what do the masses do?"*

Most go with it, according to the midwife so I gave the nod to work away.

The poor little thing squealed but calmed down soon after. First experience of pain at the age of 30 minutes!

It was time then to gather bags, check out of room 9 & check into a new part of the hospital, rest and learn how to look after our baby.

With the midwife, our bags and baby girl in a clear plastic trolley, we walk through the exit doors and I wave a goodbye to the staff. They were all new staff members and they did try and entertain my excitement. Down corridors we walked and to our left another corridor joined ours. The doors swung open just as we crossed its intersection and low and behold it is Mammy. We walk together – me walking, Mammy and baby being wheeled.

We enter the post natal clinic with its buzzing sounds and get passed over to new staff and a cool midwife Sharon.
It was the early hours of a Saturday morning and it did feel like a weekend. All days in hospital do I suppose.

" Room for 3 please".

It is mad saying goodbye to the midwife who experienced the birth with us but there's no time for nostalgia. Our new midwife was real young , really enthusiastic for us, and cool. She was the first that I liked from the beginning, since this whole process began.

She got to unwrapping the baby and encouraged the skin to skin between Mammy and baby. This helps to raise or keep the baby's temperature at normal levels and seals that bond between mother and baby, [so they say anyway].

The temperature of baby was low and the midwife did seem to be worried about that and so wrapped the baby's head, encouraged skin to skin action with the mother and she kept monitoring this. This created a mini-stress situation but after what we had been through we were ready for it.

Thankfully the baby responded and her temperature rose. The way the midwife wrapped the baby was origami at its best - we were in awe of her. At this stage you really don't have a clue what to do with the baby and the fact the professionals are there, really takes the edge off. They are the greatest people.

Soon after, it was breast feeding time. Well trial anyway. Instinct kicked in for baby and thankfully for us the trial worked. I believe that's not the same for all women and apparently freaks them out.

This first feed is not milk but collostrum. A super nutrient drink to kick start the baby. It had a yellowish colour to it. Enough said. 20 min per boob and that was that.

> *After all you've been through the fact the wife has her boobs out and they are being manoeuvred by other women into the baby's mouth does not phaze you in the slightest*

Still in awe, cuddles were next - we were happy and exhausted. We all lay down to rest – 2 hours later she settled. I texted family to announce the arrival. The wife still drugged out of it, we slept as a family for the first time.

The Post Natal Clinic:

Lots of loud buzzing noises. These are constant and initially you have no idea what they are. It sounds like a door buzzer but we found out later it is the "call button" for the patients.

The midwives come in loudly and talk at normal pitch. This is so loud when you are lying in a quiet room and so annoying if you have just managed to get asleep.

In my texts to the family I also managed to fend off any visits until way later in the day. We were all knackered. There was a roll out bed for me, trolley for baby and main bed for one exhausted and drugged-out mother.

The breakfast lady came in thick and fast and managed to be louder than the midwives and had the personality of a corn flake. I got to thinking the reason they talk so loud was to get the baby used to it. She seemed okay with it, but it did annoy us parents.

Because of the C-section my wife was to spend a few days in this room and we got to see so many staff rotate throughout their shifts, it was mental.

After breakfast, things went quiet again and we slept. Near lunch, the noises crept back in and we awoke.

The first bath was an unexpected occurrence. The baby had the biggest poo ever and managed to cover herself in it. I could tell the midwife was coming to the end of her shift as she was reluctant to change her.

The Beginning

She said she'd be back. A new midwife came along a bit later, and she took control and off we went to bath her. The poo was so stinky and sticky as it was the digested colostrum or other ingested materials while inside the uterus. [even this has a name : Meconium].

The baby was so small in the lady's hands and the midwife bathed her like a true professional. There is definitely a knack to this bathing thing and you are in awe of these women as they get to work. If I was to bath her now I would not have a clue and would probably drop or over drench the baby. There were so many cleaning steps, lotions, sprays, clothes etc etc. I wouldn't have known where to start. In the beginning, everything looks way too hard. The baby though responded to the correctly warmed water and seemed to enjoy the whole experience.

My wife missed the first bath but there would be plenty of time for that later. For now she needed to relax and recover.

The first visitors came in and of course it's family first. This part is exciting to start with. To see the reactions on their faces and to see the happiness in their eyes is something really cool. Aunties, Uncles, Grandfather & Grandmother all get their turn to introduce themselves to the new family addition. So small, so tired and so precious, the cuddling is watched with a careful eye from Mother and Father.

The midwifes are great, we get the repeating ones come in on their shifts and the new ones, aswell as the random other nurse /doctor people who come in to check temperature, oxygen [through this funny foot strap?] and red eye ? It's all hazey.

We woke at 2.45am to celebrate 1 day birthday & celebrated with sleep.

My wife is not taking as many drugs now and I initially thought this was connected to the baby being restless and crying. The more drugs Mammy has, the quieter the baby perhaps. And I tell you what, the nurses are full on with the drug pushing again. Not too sure why so much, maybe they want the baby to be quiet too.

The system of giving the drugs was exhausting too – "name check", then the superior drug pusher would sign it off and they would wait until all was ingested.

Feeding Frenzy - HELP!

The second day, the feeding frenzy starts and the baby learns what it means to be hungry. My wife was so exhausted that it felt bad to wake her everytime the baby cried for more.

I remember the second night in hospital and the baby was crying like crazy. I was walking up and down the room trying to sshh her, trying to ease her back to sleep. This went on all night. There were moments there when I was exhausted and baby is full on stereo crying, that I jumped from thoughts of *"shut up"* to *"oh the poor thing"*. To suppress the *"shut up"* part I needed to sleep when the baby did. No visitors on day 3, it needed to be done.

I was taking her for a walk around the corridors on the third morning to give my wife a break, and she started crying loudly. One of the reception btchs, [sorry but I've had it with ignorant receptionists at this point), says angrily [as the baby crying was annoying her]:

"Does that baby need feeding?"

I wish I had said : *"Is that a rhetorical question?".* I walked her back to the room then to wake my wife for milk. When the baby cries I feel stressed out. I did consider thoughts of ear plugs. Maybe daddy plugs? Another invention idea hey?

The tired excitement continued though and Mammy even needed help to shower. The visitors kept coming over the next couple of days. I soon learn to sleep while the baby sleeps - otherwise I'll get unstuck. This is the golden rule that was to apply now and well into the future.

Due to the "vaginal bypass", my wife had to be in hospital for 5 days. I started to use the visitors to my advantage and go for a walk, or go home for a bit. It was so cool to get out of the hospital, because it does get a little claustrophobic in there, after a while. The world outside was ticking along as normal and was totally oblivious to the experience and adventure we had just witnessed. We had a new gift to give the world but the world was too busy to notice. In such a busy place and surrounded by people you can feel strangely alone. Alone but a member of a bigger team. The paradoxes just keep on coming.

A few days like this and it was almost time to re-enter the Big World Proper .....

The Beginning

The Pub:

Way before we were due to have this baby, and probably while visiting the hospital for the pre-natal classes, I had my eye on this little old pub just walking distance from the hospital. I had looked forward to sitting at that bar in there and toasting my new arrival and my first baby. That day had now arrived.

Accompanied by my wife's father and step dad, I sat in that pub and listened to their wise old tales and some of their experiences as a Dad. I sat facing the bar as I sipped my last sip and I toasted to my new little girl.

It was just as I had imagined all those months ago. I wished at that moment that my own family was there to share this, but that was not to be. I dreamt of home and wished my family was here. Ironically they were. It's just a new one. I drank the very last sip of beer and walked back to the hospital. We slept one more night in there and escaped the next day to start a journey new..........

```
𝔣                              The End
𝔣𝔣
𝔣𝔣𝔣
𝔣𝔣𝔣𝔣
𝔣𝔣𝔣𝔣𝔣
𝔣𝔣𝔣𝔣𝔣𝔣
𝔣𝔣𝔣𝔣𝔣𝔣𝔣
𝔣𝔣𝔣𝔣𝔣𝔣𝔣𝔣
𝔣𝔣𝔣𝔣𝔣𝔣𝔣𝔣𝔣        Middle Earth
𝔣𝔣𝔣𝔣𝔣𝔣𝔣𝔣𝔣𝔣
𝔣𝔣𝔣𝔣𝔣𝔣𝔣𝔣𝔣𝔣𝔣
𝔣𝔣𝔣𝔣𝔣𝔣𝔣𝔣𝔣𝔣𝔣𝔣
𝔣𝔣𝔣𝔣𝔣𝔣𝔣𝔣𝔣𝔣𝔣𝔣𝔣
𝔣𝔣𝔣𝔣𝔣𝔣𝔣𝔣𝔣𝔣𝔣𝔣𝔣𝔣
𝔣𝔣𝔣𝔣𝔣𝔣𝔣𝔣𝔣𝔣𝔣𝔣𝔣𝔣𝔣
𝔣𝔣𝔣𝔣𝔣𝔣𝔣𝔣𝔣𝔣𝔣𝔣𝔣𝔣𝔣𝔣
𝔣𝔣𝔣𝔣𝔣𝔣𝔣𝔣𝔣𝔣𝔣𝔣𝔣𝔣𝔣𝔣𝔣 𝔤 The Beginning
```

For more from the Author, keep an eye out for the real Beginning:
OMGtheDiary.com

Index

Made in the USA
San Bernardino, CA
15 December 2017